# I WANT TO KNOW

This series of books sets out to present what the Bible actually teaches. We have in mind a readership made up of people of all ages who are comparatively new to the Christian faith or who are feeling their way towards it.

Inevitably, some of the topics considered may be easier to deal with than others. All those who have contributed to the series have in some way or other been involved in a teaching ministry, but in presenting this series of books we are not writing primarily for theological students. Our concern is to help people who are enquiring about the Christian faith and those who have come to believe but who have not had a Christian background. In recent years there has been a tendency to regard Christian doctrine lightly, and to emphasize Christian experience and Christian living. What is needed is a balance between the various aspects of the Christian faith, so that both our experience and our way of life may be measured against the yardstick of what the Bible teaches.

We therefore present this series in the prayerful hope that some seekers after truth may come through to a living faith, and that those whose experience of Christ is new may be built up to become mature men and women of God.

While each book stands on its own feet, we recommend that those who desire to gain a full-orbed picture of what Christianity is all about should study the series as a whole.

EDITOR

# I WANT TO KNOW

*what the Bible says about*

# GOD

## A SKEVINGTON WOOD
B.A., Ph.D., F.R.Hist.S.

*Series Editor: G. W. KIRBY M.A.*
*Formerly Principal of London Bible College*

## KINGSWAY PUBLICATIONS
EASTBOURNE

ISBN 0 86065 040 5

Unless otherwise stated, biblical quotations
are from the Revised Standard Version of the Bible,
copyright 1946, 1952, © 1971, 1973 by the
Division of Christian Education of the National Council of the
Churches of Christ in the USA.

Printed in Great Britain for
KINGSWAY PUBLICATIONS LTD
Lottbridge Drove, Eastbourne, E. Sussex BN23 6NT by
Richard Clay (The Chaucer Press) Ltd, Bungay, Suffolk

# CONTENTS

# INTRODUCTION

It was a television news report on the plight of refugees escaping from Cambodia into Thailand. The harrowing scenes of suffering and starvation, with which we have grown all too familiar in our depressing generation, filled the screen. Children reduced to skin and bone; mothers aging before their time; the old ready to drop and die, so it seemed, at any moment. A boy of twelve screamed as a bullet was removed from his leg without the aid of any anaesthetic. It was enough to move even the most indifferent at least to some measure of pity.

The commentator told viewers that he had asked a Christian missionary, who was giving what help he could, whether the tragedy of the situation did not undermine his faith in God. The missionary replied that the very reverse was the case. If such pain and deprivation was the result of human cruelty, then belief in God became even more essential. 'There must be someone better than man.'

To that missionary, God was not a problem. He was the answer. That has always been the attitude of Christians, and it has its source in what God has shown us of himself. This he has done above all in Christ, but what we know of Christ and God's prior and parallel disclosure of himself through other means is recorded in the Scriptures. It is, then, to the Bible that we turn if we want to learn about God.

What will strike us straightaway is that here the approach is always positive. Nowadays we are surrounded by negative thoughts about God. Most of our modern thinkers are puzzled by him. They find that for them he raises more difficulties than

9

he solves. They cannot even agree what the word 'God' might be taken to mean. Some would query whether it carries any freight of reality at all. What the theologians call God-talk has often led to God-denial. Things came to a head in the sixties when it was confidently reported that God was dead. The fact that he is still being discussed in the eighties suggests that his obituary notices were premature and indeed based on a misconception.

That is not at all surprising to those who believe in the God of the Bible. He cannot be disposed of so conveniently as the sceptics would like to suppose. He is by nature the living and eternal God and no attempt of man to disprove his existence will ever succeed.

For the Christian, however, it is not enough merely to be convinced that God is. He will want also to discover who God is, and this will involve a search of the Scriptures. In the successive chapters of this book we will be undertaking what John Robinson calls an 'exploration into God'.

It will prove rewarding only to those who tackle it with serious intent. If we are to know God we must mean business and be prepared to gird up the loins of our mind as we trace the track of divine truth. 'To believe in God,' according to the Spanish writer Miguel de Unamuno, 'is to long for his existence and, further, it is to act as if he existed; it is to live by the longing and to make it the inner spring of our actions.' We can go much further than that. To believe in God is to know that he exists and to act in obedience to him because he exists. It is to live by this assurance and to prove in experience that the indwelling God himself becomes the inner spring of all our doing and being.

People sometimes speak about 'the quest for God'. That can be a misleading expression. It might suggest that God is lost and has to be found. It could imply that he is remote and inaccessible. As we shall see, the Bible tells us differently. It is man who is lost and God who is searching for him. In Christ, the infinitely majestic God has drawn near to us and made contact. Our response must be to follow the clues he has given in his word and allow him to crown his quest for us by introducing himself as far as we are capable of comprehending him by faith.

# 1

# THE BEING OF GOD

'If God did not exist,' claimed Voltaire, that unconventional French thinker, 'it would be necessary to invent him.' He felt that such a belief was essential to keep people sane. If there is no God, then life loses all meaning and there seems to be no alternative to stark despair.

That is clearly how the Bible looks at the issue. It refuses to argue for the existence of God. It simply assumes that he is there. 'In the beginning God...' (Genesis 1:1). On the other hand, Scripture does not ignore the fact that some may doubt and even deny his being. 'The fool says in his heart, "There is no God"' (Psalm 14:1). His rash conclusion reflects the extent of his folly. Who is he with his tiny mind to decide whether or not God exists? To imagine that human reason is in itself capable of determining the truth of the matter is nothing short of impudence – and that is what is implied by the Hebrew word translated as fool.

To dispute or dismiss the existence of God is more than foolish, however. According to another psalm, it is iniquitous. It is 'the wicked man' who in his self-obsessed arrogance renounces the Lord and is not concerned to seek him. 'All his thoughts are, "There is no God"' (Psalm 10:4). 'An atheist does not find God,' explained Wendell Baxter, 'for the same reason that a thief does not find a policeman. He is not looking for him.'

Those who bluntly repudiate any notion of God's existence, however, are in a minority even among sceptics. There are more who would insist that we cannot know. That is the strict meaning of agnosticism. It is more than simply a matter of responding with a 'Don't know' to any Gallup poll enquiry about whether there is a God. Thorough-going agnosticism takes the matter much further. It concludes quite emphatically that the problem is insoluble. On this view, if God does exist at all, he is unknowable. He is far too great to disclose himself.

Now that may perhaps sound to us like modesty, but it actually amounts to a form of conceit similar to that which dismisses the reality of God altogether. It is a most sweeping assertion to claim that God cannot be known. As Blaise Pascal – scientist, philosopher and Christian – once put it: 'If you say that man is too little for God to speak to him, you must be very big to be able to judge.'

The Bible does not for a moment suggest that we can learn all about God and thus capture him, as it were, within our own system of thought. But it does tell us that we may discover as much about him as he chooses to reveal. Those who accept his manifestation of himself in Christ will come to know him best, but no one need be shut off from him. Paul reminds the Christians in Rome that even men who stifle the truth by their wickedness must not resort to the excuse that they have no knowledge of God. 'For what can be known about God is plain to them, because God has shown it to them' (Romans 1:19).

It used to be the fashion to set out a series of proofs to demonstrate the existence of God. Nowadays we are more reluctant to make any such attempt, since the Bible does not do so either. Logic can neither prove nor disprove the reality of God. In the long run it is only by faith that we become convinced, 'For whoever would draw near to God must believe that he exists and that he rewards those who seek him' (Hebrews 11:6). So instead of relying on arguments for the existence of God, it is better to regard the same factors simply as considerations which confirm faith. In themselves they will not necessarily persuade the sceptical, but at least they enable the Christian to show that there are reasons to support his belief.

## Cause and effect in the universe

In the first place he will want to draw attention to the universe in which we live as citizens of planet Earth. No one disputes the fact that it exists and that we find ourselves in it. But where does it come from? How do we account for it all? Did it just grow like Topsy or must we look for some prior factor to explain its existence?

This line of reasoning is usually labelled 'cosmological', because it has to do with the 'cosmos' or universe. Sometimes it has been mistakenly assumed that 'cosmos' is connected with cause, which is not the case. What used to be called the cosmological argument is simply that which starts from the undeniable fact that there is a cosmos.

The element of cause does nevertheless feature in this consideration, for we take it for granted both scientifically and in practical everyday life that no event can be produced without a cause. The uncaused emergence of any substance or phenomenon has never yet been observed. The sequence of cause and effect is a law of the universe. If that is the case, must it not also apply to the origin of the universe in which it operates? Either everything just happened without any previous existence of any kind, or there was some first cause which lay behind it all. The Bible equates this with the being of God, who is the Creator of all things.

If something now exists it has either emerged from nothing or it has a source. Unless we are to assume that this vast and complex universe had its origin in a vacuum, we are compelled to conclude that it came from what had existed before the beginning of time and space, and from what must therefore be eternal. The Christian who believes in God as Creator vindicates his conviction by enquiring whether it is not more probable that the universe should have been produced by a conscious personal intelligence rather than as a result of what the German idealist Artur Schopenhauer called 'blind will'.

## Evidence of design

As a second consideration which confirms faith, the Christian will point to the evidence of design to be discerned throughout the universe. Space exploration in recent years has served to expand and strengthen this impression. There is every indication of a coherent pattern. Indeed, without this consistency science would be unable to establish its theories and formulate its principles. This is an extension of the argument from cause and effect. A particular kind of effect must have a particular kind of cause. If there are signs of order and purpose in the cosmos, does this not presuppose a mind and a plan behind the phenomena of nature?

Edwin Orr was once walking along a Queensland beach, lost in contemplation, when he came on a pool of water in the exact shape of Australia. He did not give it much thought, for he took it to be a coincidental effect of the outgoing tide. Ten paces away, however, he found another map of Australia, and another and another. He was now compelled to find an explanation for the sequence. It did not surprise him to discover that a boy with a bucket and spade was responsible.

'The heavens are telling the glory of God; and the firmament proclaims his handiwork,' declares the psalmist (Psalm 19:1). The apostle Paul explains in Romans that 'ever since the creation of the world' God's 'invisible nature, namely, his eternal power and deity, has been clearly perceived in the things that have been made' (Romans 1:20). The same conclusion is drawn from the evidence of design in the personality of man himself. 'He who planted the ear, does he not hear? He who formed the eye, does he not see?' (Psalm 94:9).

## Moral awareness

In the third place the Christian finds corroboration of his belief in God's being as he thinks about man's moral awareness. By this is meant the fact that he has a built-in sense of right and wrong. The apostle Paul explains that those who have not received the law as the Jews have done (and we could now add, those who have not received the gospel as Christians have done) are nevertheless conscious that a standard of behaviour is demanded from them. 'What the law requires is written on their hearts, while their conscience also bears witness and their conflicting thoughts accuse or perhaps excuse them' (Romans 2:15).

What the philosopher Kant called 'the moral law within' is in itself an evidence of God's existence, as he was not slow to recognize. The modern attempt to account for conscience in purely sociological terms fails to do justice to the facts. The Bible regards conscience as coming from above and apart from man, as well as being an element within him. It is inborn and universal. It is not simply the product of environment or education or race impression. It is God's arbiter within, or, as Cardinal Newman described it, 'the aboriginal Vicar of Christ in the soul'.

## Religious consciousness

If a realization of moral values is common to every stage of human history, so also is an awareness of the divine. Man is incurably religious. Belief in a god of some sort is so general and so compelling that it amounts almost to an instinct. It finds expression in cult and ritual, in prayer and devotion from the most primitive to highly developed forms. In his speech before the court of the Areopagus in Athens – representing the top-level intellectuals of Greece – the apostle Paul noted that the many shrines and statues in the city reflected a universal search for God. Indeed in every nation under the sun men 'seek God, in the hope that they might feel after him and find him' (Acts 17:27). 'Even among pagans,' comments Professor E. J. Young, 'there has remained the persuasion that God exists,' and he refers to the fact that the astrologers at the court of King Nebuchadnezzar in Babylon knew about deities 'whose dwelling is not with flesh' (Daniel 2:11; cf. Romans 1:19).

Is all this no more than a massive delusion? Does it represent a one-sided exercise with no corresponding reality as its ultimate goal? Man has been defined as a worshipping animal. But what a pathetic farce life would turn out to be unless the object of his age-long yearning is as real as himself. There are many today who fail to find any meaning at all in the procession of events because they have lost the key. That key is belief in God, and without it all is chaos and confusion.

The Bible assures us that man's quest is far from futile. 'You will seek me and find me; when you seek me with all your heart, I will be found by you, says the LORD' (Jeremiah 29:13–14). God is not mocked, nor does he mock us. When we respond to the universal urge to make contact with a power beyond ourselves, we are not setting out on a wild-goose chase. There is someone to be discovered.

## The idea of God

A further consideration which confirms faith has to do even more directly with the being of God as such. It argues from the idea of divine being to its reality. Could man ever have conceived of God at all if he did not exist? Or, to put it another way, there is, as we have seen, a widespread notion that a being like God is to be found. What is the explanation of this impression? Is it not so transcendent that only God himself could have led man to think of it?

It may be (and has been) objected that because I happen to entertain the idea of a ten pound note in my wallet this does not necessarily prove that I have one. Such a criticism misses the point, however, for what is at issue is the existence of ten pound notes and wallets to keep them in, rather than my possession of them.

In any case, it would be foolish to claim that every product of man's fertile imagination has its precise counterpart in reality. Plainly this is not so. But the idea of a sovereign God is so commanding and so exalted that the Bible insists that it is altogether beyond what man might possibly have conjured up

unaided. Man could never have known God at all unless God
had chosen to reveal himself. If this is so, then the fact that
man does know something about God is a confirmation of his
existence.

Such, then, are some of the considerations which confirm
faith. As we have seen, they do not amount to knock-down
proofs, for the existence of God can neither be established nor
assailed by any such methods. In the nature of the case, belief
in God is a matter of faith. In a sense faith would no longer
be faith if it demanded an indisputable demonstration.

None of the foregoing lines of reasoning will completely
convince the unbeliever, and we must not expect them to do
so. But if as Christians we are asked to provide some logical
grounds for our belief in a God who is, then these are the
traditional answers. As Herman Bavinck, that outstanding
Dutch theologian of the last generation, used to express it,
although the classical arguments for the existence of God are
weak as proofs, they are nevertheless strong as testimonies. They
are not sources but products of faith. They represent the witness
of those who have found it possible to believe in God. The
Bible itself does not even begin to make out a systematic case
to show that God is real. It simply records his revelation of
himself and the depositions of those who have encountered him
in experience. That is why the Christian does not need to prove
that God is. He knows beyond the shadow of doubt, because
he has met him in Christ. 'And this is eternal life, that they
know thee the only true God, and Jesus Christ whom thou hast
sent' (John 17:3). That was how Jesus prayed to his Father,
and there lies the final assurance that God exists.

Here is how a distinguished scientist, Sir Arthur Eddington,
once summed up the matter.

In the case of our human friends we take their existence for granted,
not caring whether it is proven or not. Our relationship is such
that we could read philosophical arguments designed to prove the
non-existence of each other and perhaps even be convinced by them
– and then laugh together over so odd a conclusion. I think it is

something of the same kind of security we should seek in our relationship with God. The most flawless proof of the existence of God is no substitute for it: and if we have that relationship the most convincing disproof is turned harmlessly aside.

Believers are convinced, like Daniel, without the need for elaborate arguments that 'there is a God in heaven' (Daniel 2:28).

# 2

# THE PERSONALITY OF GOD

In discussing the existence of God in the previous chapter, we have asked the question 'Is he?' 'Is there such a one as God?' 'Is he real?' We have seen that the Bible does not deal directly with the way in which the existence of God might be substantiated. It prefers to recognize his presence without pausing to prove it, on the assumption that 'the people who know their God' (Daniel 11:32) do not need to buttress their faith and experience with such arguments.

In referring to God as *he*, in the enquiries we have made about his being, we have already presumed (as the Bible itself does) that God is personal. That is to say, he is not *it* but *he*. There are some nowadays who would raise the objection that to use such terms is to beg the question from the start. Do we not first of all need to make out a case for the personality or personhood of God, before we allow ourselves to speak about 'him' in such a fashion?

## Rejection of a personal God

There is nothing new in the contemporary rejection of a personal God. Thinkers in the past have expressed similar doubts. They accept the argument for a first cause to account for the universe in which we are placed, but they regard it as altogether impersonal. In a recent Gallup poll in Britain, 29% confessed belief in a personal God, but 35% reported that they tended to think of a spirit or life-force as operating behind the scenes. Incidentally, only 6% rejected the idea altogether, whereas predictably 18% admitted that they did not know. Clearly then, those who want to acknowledge God have difficulty nevertheless in recognizing him as personal.

Others identify the world with God. There is no God but the universe itself, so they would have us believe. Beyond and outside it he does not exist. This inadequate view is known as pantheism. Everything is God and God is everything. God has no independent being. And if God is not to be distinguished from the world, and the world in turn is not to be distinguished from God, then the pantheist's deity is no more than an *it*. No personality is possible. It does not know itself. Only man can know it.

Others again go so far as to conceive of God as the personification of an abstract idea. 'God' has to be included within inverted commas to indicate that the name is merely a symbol. It is a convenient piece of sign language. Psychologically, it represents the projection of man's own features on to the screen of the divine. It has been observed that, whereas it was once believed that God created man in his own image, the situation is now reversed and man has created God in a human image. However, although man is himself a personal being, the identi-kit picture he has drawn of God is no more than a notion in his head and falls far short of what Scripture means when it points to an authentically personal God.

In the Bible God is never *it* and always *he*. Nor is this a later development evolved out of some more primitive idea of a God who is rather less than personal. 'Unquestionably the most distinct and strongly marked conception in regard to God in the Old Testament is that of his personality,' according to Professor A. B. Davidson. From the first historical references to God in Scripture he is fully recognized as a person.

## God is distinct from creation

Nowhere is God at all confused with nature. He is, of course, concerned for his creation and in that sense involved in it. But he is always distinct from it and unambiguously personal in his being. In the opening chapter of Genesis, God stands over against nature and expresses his opinion of it: 'And God saw everything that he had made, and behold, it was very good' (Genesis 1:31). He stands over against man and requires obedience to his commands: 'You may freely eat of every tree of the garden; but of the tree of the knowledge of good and evil you shall not eat, for in the day that you eat of it you shall die' (Genesis 2:16–17). It is not that man may know God, but God does not know man – as pantheism is compelled to concede. The boot is on the other foot. The Bible teaches that God knows man, but that man could not know God unless God had graciously chosen to reveal himself.

God, then, is separate from the universe he has made. The creator is not part of his creation. He superintends the processes of the natural world, but he is not locked up in them. 'He covers the heavens with clouds, he prepares rain for the earth, he makes grass grow upon the hills. He gives to the beasts their food, and to the young ravens which cry' (Psalm 147:8–9). God's control is not remote; yet on the other hand, he is sovereign over nature and not imprisoned by it.

## Marks of personality

We must now proceed to consider the marks of personality in God as they are described in Scripture. What is it about God which shows him to be a person? Immediately we face a problem, for how do we know what we are looking for? We have no other criterion of personality than our own. That is to say, we can only tell from ourselves as human beings what it means to be a person, for we have never come into contact with any other sort of person, let alone one who is divine.

It needs to be recognized from the start, therefore, that personhood in God rises far above what it is in man. Yet the comparison still remains valid, since the Bible informs us that man was made in the image of God and after his likeness (Genesis 1:26; cf. verse 27). What we understand by being a person is what marks off man from even the animal creation and at the same time reflects his divine origin. It is the Maker's own stamp and signature.

It is thus legitimate to infer from the personality of man that God himself is personal, as well as to derive the criteria from the same source. If we ourselves are persons, where did we come from? Surely we cannot be greater than the God who made us? Since we are personal beings, it is apparent that he must be such as well. Hence, from our own personhood we can rightly make the deduction that the God from whom we came is personal too.

## Self-consciousness

The first mark of personality which we must list is self-consciousness. Man is aware of himself. He is what the French philosopher René Descartes dubbed 'a thinking being'. He has the capacity to escape from inside his own skin, as it were, and take an objective view of himself. This distinctive feature of the human species – for self-consciousness is more than mere consciousness, which other creatures share – is derived from God himself. He is essentially the one who knows who he is and what he is doing. That is why he can describe himself in terms of his own self-consciousness as 'I AM WHO I AM' (Exodus 3:14).

A recurring phrase in the Scriptures of the Old Testament is 'By myself I have sworn' (Genesis 22:16; Isaiah 45:23; cf. Jeremiah 22:5; 49:13; Exodus 32:13). God is not only aware of himself as existent, but also of what character he bears. Because he is who he is, then what he does can be relied on. His ultimate appeal is to himself. He can swear by nothing greater, for he is supreme.

The uniqueness of God is implied in this evidence of his personality. He is not merely one of a class. He is in a class of his own. Even though personhood is bestowed on man in the act of creation, God himself remains essentially other than man. He is not just a person among many others. He is a unique person. Indeed, it may be more accurate to say that he is person.

All persons derive their personality from his person, but he himself is the prototype. Human personality even at best is but a pale reflection of the divine.

'To whom then will you liken God, or what likeness compare with him?' asks the prophet Isaiah (40:18). He is so immeasurably superior to the useless idols of the nations surrounding Israel that he can laugh them to scorn. 'To whom then will you compare me, that I should be like him? says the Holy One' (Isaiah 40:25). God himself is aware of his own supremacy. And again: 'To whom will you liken me and make me equal, and compare me, that we may be alike?' (Isaiah 46:5). The answer, of course, is no one. The person of God is altogether unique. 'I am God, and there is no other; I am God, and there is none like me' (Isaiah 46:9). The theologians talk about the singularity of God, or his 'in himselfness'. By this they mean that he not only knows himself but knows himself to be incomparable.

## Self-determination

A further feature of personality as we find it expressed in man is will or self-determination. In the language of Shakespeare, he is 'a free determinator 'twixt right and wrong'. He has been endowed with the ability to choose. He can decide whether he does this or that. The Bible makes it plain that this freedom has been severely limited by the Fall of mankind, but it still remains and can be exercised in the everyday situations of life. A person is someone with a will of his own.

God is the one with whom self-determination originated. His is the primal will. Had he not willed man, then man would never have been created. All wills therefore stem from the divine will, although not all are now subservient to it. 'I know that thou canst do all things,' Job confesses to the Lord at the close of his epic encounter, 'and that no purpose of thine can be thwarted' (Job 42:2).

The sovereignty of God is a major theme of Scripture. The concept of his kingship is firmly embedded in the biblical tradition. 'I am the LORD, your Holy One, the Creator of Israel, your King' (Isaiah 43:15). 'Thus says the LORD, the King of Israel and his Redeemer, the LORD of hosts: I am the first and I am the last; besides me there is no god' (Isaiah 44:6). 'The King of Israel, the LORD is in your midst; you shall fear evil no more' (Zephaniah 3:15).

The same truth is expressed in terms not only of monarchy but also of majesty, which really means greatness. 'The LORD reigns; he is robed in majesty; the LORD is robed, he is girded with strength. . . . Thy throne is established from of old' (Psalm 93:1–2). 'Bless the LORD, O my soul! O LORD my God, thou art very great! Thou art clothed with honour and majesty' (Psalm 104:1). Another psalm speaks about 'the glorious splendour of thy majesty' (Psalm 145:5) and again about 'the glory of thy kingdom' (verse 11). Isaiah refers to 'the glory of his majesty' (2:10, 19, 21) and 'the majesty of the LORD' (24:14). Micah prophesies that the Messiah will 'stand and feed his flock in the strength of the LORD, in the majesty of the name of the LORD his God' (Micah 5:4). In the letter to the Hebrews the phrase 'the Majesty on high [in heaven]' is used on two occasions as signifying God himself (Hebrews 1:3; 8:1).

In the exercise of his sovereign will, then, God reveals himself as a personal being. He is always in control. He decides what is to be and what is not to be. His will is subject to no one and subjects all.

## Action

But God not only wills to do. He actually does what he wills. That is a further indication of his personality. In man the ability to do what is willed is curtailed. Sin prevents him from performing the good he approves or avoiding the evil he deplores, as the apostle Paul discovered in agonizing experience (Romans 7:15–21). There is no such restriction in God. All that he aims to do, he perfectly accomplishes. There is no great gulf fixed between the will and the deed, as there is in man. With God, willing and acting are one. 'He is unchangeable and who can turn him? What he desires, that he does' (Job 23:13). It is because of this correspondence between the will and its fulfilment that Job can give expression to the assurance that 'he will complete what he appoints for me; and many such things are in his mind' (verse 14).

God's action is often depicted in human terms, especially in the Old Testament. For example, he 'stretches out his hand' against those with whom he is displeased (Isaiah 5:25; Jeremiah 51:25; Ezekiel 6:14; 35:3), or he 'bares his holy arm' before the eyes of all the nations (Isaiah 52:10). This is not to say that God is no more than a man blown up into a deity, but it does confirm the fact of his personality. We can use no other language than that which is applicable to a man if we are to convey how God goes into action.

## Relationship

That God is personal is also obvious from the fact that he can enter into a relationship with man. He seeks communion with him, and that is only possible between persons. How do we form a human relationship? It is by speaking and listening, by experiencing the pressure of one will upon another, and ultimately by the giving of self in outgoing love. This, of course, is our relationship with God, but only because first of all it is his relationship with us. He does what only a person can. He speaks. He visits us. He commands. He loves. 'Perhaps the root of personality is capacity for affection,' suggested R. C. Moberly, and surely he is right. A loving God must be a personal God, and 'God is love' (1 John 4:8, 16).

## Manifested in a person

The final and determinative corroboration of God's personality is the fact that he has manifested himself in the person of his Son. In Christ God came to live in a human life. 'In Christ God was reconciling the world to himself,' as Paul informs the Christians in Corinth (2 Corinthians 5:19). Only a person could express himself through a person. If God were not personal, the person of Christ would not have been either a possible or a suitable means of making himself known to mankind. 'We can give a conclusive reason for affirming the personality of God,' claimed Professor Hugh Ross Mackintosh. 'We can say: it is in this character he encounters us in Christ, the great Doer of redeeming things.'

There are some who might be inclined to object that to regard God as personal implies a necessary limitation. Such a hesitation could only arise from a consideration of personality as it is to be found in human samples. The limitation is a result of human imperfection. We may properly conclude that God himself as the Absolute possesses personality in all its fullness, without flaw or hindrance.

The untrammelled expression of divine personality helps us to realize that the enigma of the Trinity underlines the infinite difference between God and man. According to the biblical revelation, God is not only personal: his personhood expands itself in terms of three beings who are equally himself as well as altogether themselves – the Father, the Son, and the Holy Spirit. The unique nature of God's personality is nowhere more evident than in this mysterious three-in-oneness.

# 3

# THE ONENESS OF GOD

William Temple, former Archbishop of Canterbury, once strikingly claimed that it is as much idolatry to worship a false mental image of God as a false metal image. In western civilization today we may not be guilty of bowing down before what the Bible calls molten images or pagan gods of wood and stone, but we are all too frequently found prostrating ourselves in front of some distorted conception of who God is and thus succumbing to the idolatry of the mind.

We have already considered several of these deviant views of God – the idea that he does not exist at all (atheism), the idea that he cannot be known (agnosticism), and the idea that he is no more than the sum total of the physical universe (pantheism). Far more common, however, throughout the course of history, and in many parts of the world, is polytheism – that is, the recognition of many gods.

Over against atheism, the Bible affirms the being of God. Over against agnosticism, the Bible insists that God is knowable since he has chosen to reveal himself. Over against pantheism, the Bible witnesses to the personality of God in distinction from what he has created. Over against polytheism, the Bible asserts the oneness, or unity, of God.

## One God

According to Scripture, there is only one God. That is the basic creed of the Old Testament. 'Hear, O Israel: The LORD our God is one LORD' (Deuteronomy 6:4). Here is a positive declara-

tion of what is stated negatively in the first of the ten commandments: 'I am the LORD your God, who brought you out of the
land of Egypt, out of the house of bondage. You shall have
no other gods before me' (Exodus 20:2–3). The Hebrew phrase
in the passage from Deuteronomy is literally 'The LORD our
God the LORD one'. As the footnotes in the Revised Standard
Version indicate, there are several ways in which it might be
translated. It could be 'the LORD our God, the LORD is one'
or 'the LORD is our God, the LORD is one'.

Whichever rendering is preferred, the emphasis is the same.
The deity is not to be thought of as being simply one among
many. He is the only God. The divine nature, unlike ours, is
not distributed through or realized in a class or group. Men
and women are all of them members of the human species. God
is not to be regarded as belonging as it were to the divine species,
along with scores and hundreds of other deities. He is not only
one of a kind: he is the only one of his kind. The Bible does
not speak about him as being the greatest of all gods. It does
not recognize any other gods at all. The one God has no rivals.
However real they may seem to their devotees, the pagan deities
are non-starters. In the sight of the one true God, they have
no substance at all.

'"See now that I, even I, am he, and there is no god beside
me"' – this is from the song of Moses – '"I kill and I make
alive; I wound and I heal; and there is none that can deliver
out of my hand"' (Deuteronomy 32:39). God's ability to rescue
his people and scatter their enemies depends on his uniqueness.
It is because he is the one only true God that he can unloose
the lightning of his terrible swift sword (cf. verse 41). So
Hannah, the mother of the prophet Samuel, can exult in the
Lord and rejoice in his salvation as she testifies that 'there is
none holy like the LORD, there is none besides thee; there is
no rock like our God' (1 Samuel 2:2).

## A matter of belief

There are several features to be noted in what the Bible teaches about the oneness of God. It is first a matter of belief. We have already looked at the fundamental affirmation of the Old Testament in Deuteronomy 6:4. That passage was regularly recited as containing the heart of the faith, and represents the quintessence of Judaism to this day. This conviction about the oneness of God was born out of experience when Israel was rescued from Egypt. That is made clear in the first commandment. It is also reflected in the appeal Moses made to the Israelites at the close of his first address, as recorded in the book of Deuteronomy. The second part of the exhortation in chapter 4, verses 32–40, underlines the importance of the commandment: 'You shall have no other gods before me' (Deuteronomy 5:7; cf. Exodus 20:3). As the margin helps us to understand, 'before' is really 'besides' or 'apart from'.

As a result of all that was done so unmistakably in the deliverance from Egypt, the Israelites came to believe that there is only one God. 'To you it was shown, that you might know that the LORD is God; there is no other besides him' (Deuteronomy 4:35). And again in verse 39: 'Know therefore this day, and lay it to your heart, that the LORD is God in heaven above and on the earth beneath; there is no other.' The same theme is repeated throughout the Old Testament Scriptures: 'I am the LORD, and there is no other, besides me there is no God' (Isaiah 45:5; cf. 45:18, 21). Even other nations will acknowledge the truth of God's uniqueness. 'The wealth of Egypt and the merchandise of Ethiopia, and the Sabeans, men of stature, shall come over to you and be yours, they shall follow you; they shall come over in chains and bow down to you. They will make supplication to you, saying: "God is with you only, and there is no other, no god besides him"' (Isaiah 45:14).

In the New Testament we are led on to learn that this one God meets us in three persons – Father, Son, and Holy Spirit. But this further disclosure is in no way intended to jeopardize the fact of God's unity. Indeed it is based on it and flows from it. So Paul can remind the Christians in Corinth of what they already know, namely that 'there is no God but one' (1 Corinthians 8:4; Deuteronomy 6:4). 'For although there may be so-called gods in heaven or on earth – as indeed there are many 'gods' and many 'lords' – yet for us there is one God, the Father, from whom are all things and for whom we exist, and one Lord, Jesus Christ, through whom are all things and through whom we exist' (1 Corinthians 8:5–6). And as he lists seven significant Christian unities in his Ephesian letter, the apostle includes 'one God and Father of us all, who is above all and through all and in all' (Ephesians 4:6). So in writing to Timothy, his 'son in the gospel', Paul can say (1 Timothy 1:17): 'To the King of ages, immortal, invisible, the only God, be honour and glory for ever and ever. Amen.' Such a God is the only God, explains Dr William Hendriksen,

> not merely in the coldly abstract sense that numerically there is but *one* God, but in the warm scriptural sense, namely, that this *one* God is 'unique, incomparable, glorious, loving' (Deuteronomy 6:4, 5; Isaiah 40:12–31; Romans 16:27; 1 Corinthians 8:4, 5).

## A matter of experience

The Bible also makes it clear that the oneness of God is a matter of experience. That is suggested by the comments of Dr Hendriksen quoted at the end of the last paragraph. When we recite the creed and affirm, 'I believe in one God,' we are not repeating a mathematical formula. Nor are we simply making a statement about what our minds have grasped from Scripture concerning the nature of God. 'I believe' means more than intellectual assent. It implies personal trust. We find in our own experience that God is the only one. Indeed, unless we give him the place of supremacy in our lives that he demands and deserves because he is the one true God, then the profession of our lips is hollow and insincere.

'Who is like thee, O LORD, among the gods?' enquired Moses. 'Who is like thee, majestic in holiness, terrible in glorious deeds, doing wonders?' (Exodus 15:11). The answer is, of course, that no one can be compared with God. The children of Israel knew this to be so because he had proved it when he took them out of Egypt and routed the enemy at the Red Sea. 'Thou didst stretch out thy right hand, the earth swallowed them' (verse 12). But 'thou hast led in thy steadfast love the people whom thou hast redeemed, thou hast guided them by thy strength to thy holy abode' (verse 13). It is this realization in experience that God is the only deliverer which confirms their belief in his oneness.

The inadequacy of bare belief unmatched by personal commitment is borne out by a passage in the letter of James. The writer is expounding his central theme – namely that so-called faith which does not issue in good works is lifeless. It is not enough to say that we are believers. Words need to be backed by deeds to prove them. That is what non-Christians are constantly demanding from those who profess to belong to Christ. 'Don't tell me: show me!'

What good is it for someone to claim that he has faith, asks the apostle James, if his actions do not prove it? (James 2:14). Can faith of that sort, unsupported by any practical evidence, do him any good? It is not real faith at all if it fails to lead to action. It is dead and useless. Someone may object that people are different: one man has faith, another goes in for actions. But it is not a question of one or the other. Faith and actions belong together. 'Show me how anyone can have faith without actions,' he asks. 'I will show you my faith by my actions' (verse 18, Good News Bible).

Then James goes on to address those who make a profession of faith but produce little evidence of it in their lives. 'You believe that God is one: you do well. Even the demons believe – and shudder.' Of course it is a good thing to stand up and confess our belief in the oneness of God. But the pious mouthing of such an affirmation, however orthodox it may be, is altogether worthless unless it is confirmed in experience. Why, even the demons acknowledge that God is supreme. But they nevertheless refuse to submit to his sway. They may tremble, but they do not yield. Recognition that God is one must pass from the area of assent to the area of consent if it is to be authenticated as genuine. Calvin once said that knowing about God can no more connect a man with God in a vital relationship than the sight of the sun can carry him up to heaven.

## A matter of worship

The Bible further suggests that the oneness of God is a matter of worship. When we recognize in our own experience that he is the only one, then our response will be that of adoration and thanksgiving. We shall want to bow before him in humble reverence, for that is the heart of vital worship. 'There is none like thee, O Lord; thou art great, and thy name is great in might. Who would not fear thee, O King of the nations? For this is thy due' (Jeremiah 10:6-7).

Then, when we have prostrated ourselves before God's awesome majesty, we can stand to our feet and shout his praise. The psalmist invites all who occupy this planet earth to glorify God – rulers and ruled, young men and girls, old men and children – 'let them praise the name of the Lord, for his name alone is exalted' (Psalm 148:13).

In what we have described as the basic creed of the Old Testament, recorded in the book of Deuteronomy, the affirmation of faith in one God is linked with an injunction to love. 'Hear, O Israel: the Lord our God is one Lord; and you shall love the Lord your God with all your heart, and with all your soul, and with all your might' (Deuteronomy 6:4-5). Love is a matter of experience, but it is also an expression of worship.

When one of the Jewish scribes asked Jesus, 'Which commandment is the first of all?' our Lord referred without hesitation to that passage from Deuteronomy, which the Jews knew as the *Shema*. He added a second, from Leviticus 19:18 – 'You shall love your neighbour as yourself.' 'There is no other commandment greater than these,' declared Jesus (Mark 12:31). The scribe could do no other than agree with him. 'You are right, Teacher; you have truly said that he is one, and there is no other but he; and to love him with all the heart, and with all the understanding, and with all the strength, and to love one's neighbour as oneself, is much more than all whole burnt offerings and sacrifices' (verses 32–33). In other words, the true worship of God lies not in ritual and ceremonial, but in the offering of love.

In Scripture, worship belongs only to God. It is not on any account to be directed to men. Such blasphemy is expressly and sternly forbidden. When, after a cripple had been healed, the excited crowds at Lystra wanted to offer sacrifice to Paul and Barnabas because they thought the missionaries were gods in disguise, the apostles tore their clothes in horror. They had to make it clear that they were only human like anyone else, and that worship was not to be directed to them but only to the 'living God who made the heaven and the earth and the sea and all that is in them' (Acts 14:15). Not even angels are to be worshipped (Colossians 2:18; Revelation 19:10; 22:8–9). No one but God himself is worthy. The consistent command of Scripture is to worship God and him alone.

The message of the Bible about the oneness of God represents a great simplification. In the ancient world there were gods galore. Few devotees knew which was the right one to approach in a particular situation. It was good news to find that there was only one God to please and to address in prayer. That is still the attraction of the gospel. The Christian faith is appealingly simple in what it offers to the world when compared with the complexities of the cults or fashionable philosophies. 'For there is one God,' Paul tells Timothy, as he summarizes the message he was appointed to preach: 'and there is one mediator between God and men, the man Christ Jesus' (1 Timothy 2:5).

# 4

# THE REVELATION OF GOD

The Bible not only assures us that there is a God and that we may get to know something of him. It also tells us how and where he may be known. The plain fact of the matter is that he himself is the only source of information. In the nature of the case, man can know nothing about God except what God chooses to divulge. If God had decided to keep himself to himself, then he would have remained a total enigma to man. Only because he opens himself to our understanding in love and grace can we have any reliable picture of him at all.

The self-disclosure on the part of God is labelled revelation. Unless God had revealed himself, man would still be ignorant about him. The title of a modern book asks *Has Christianity a Revelation?* It might be more accurate to say that Christianity *is* a revelation. There is nothing that we have not received (1 Corinthians 4:7). The element of 'givenness' runs through everything that belongs to the Christian faith. Our knowledge of God cannot at any point be equated with human discovery, since the very faculties by which we can take hold of what God pleases to unfold about himself are themselves bestowed by him.

## The meaning of revelation

Theologians used to distinguish between natural and revealed religion, but now we realize that everything is revealed. So we prefer to speak instead about general and special revelation. General revelation includes what God makes known of himself through nature, conscience and secular history. Special revelation is his self-disclosure in sacred history (pre-Israelite, Israelite and Christian history), in Scripture and in Christ. It is these sources of revelation that we must examine, remembering that they all represent God's voluntary communication of himself to men. Any authentic knowledge of what is divine can only come from him who is divine. That is why Ambrose of Milan could ask in the fourth century, 'To whom shall I give greater credit concerning God than God himself?' That is why Emil Brunner, the Swiss scholar, could affirm in the twentieth century, 'Through God alone God is known.'

Revelation is not only a biblical doctrine but also a biblical term. It appears both as a noun – as in the title of the last New Testament book – and as the verb to reveal. It has to do with the unveiling of what has previously been hidden and hence represents an active communication of God to men. Sometimes the reference is to the return of Christ at the end of the age (1 Corinthians 1:7; 2 Thessalonians 1:7; 1 Peter 1:7, 13), but its broader and more usual application is to the disclosure of truth about God.

After his preaching and miracles in Galilee had failed to produce the response of faith, Jesus warned the cities which did not repent that in the end Tyre and Sidon, and even Sodom and Gomorrah, would fare more favourably in the day of judgement than those who had rejected their Messiah. Then we read: 'At that time' – and what a significant juncture it was! – 'Jesus declared, "I thank thee, Father, Lord of heaven and earth, that thou hast hidden these things from the wise and understanding and revealed them to babes; yea, Father, for such was thy gracious will"' (Matthew 11:25–26). Then he went on: '"All things have been delivered to me by my Father; and no one knows the Son except the Father, and no one knows the Father except the Son and any one to whom the Son chooses to reveal him"' (verse 27). The Father, then, is the source of revelation, but the Son is the supreme medium, as we shall see. The contrast in this section of Matthew, however, is between those who have a reputation for wisdom, according to the standards of this world (like the scribes and Pharisees), and those who are innocents in the eyes of the sophisticated (like the tax-collectors and other social outcasts) who have nevertheless accepted the message of Jesus. The knowledge of God, then, is hidden from those who fancy that they are the experts, and revealed to the simple-hearted.

That is why, when Paul is dealing with the same paradox in the opening chapter of 1 Corinthians, he quotes an appropriate verse from Isaiah's prophecy: 'I will destroy the wisdom of the wise, and the cleverness of the clever I will thwart' (1 Corinthians 1:19; cf. Isaiah 29:14). Human wisdom on its own is incapable of grasping divine truth. God makes himself known to those who, like children, are eagerly waiting for enlightenment.

## The revelation of God in nature

The first area of God's general revelation is nature. Despite the effects of the Fall, the world around us still carries its Maker's mark. As the Lakeland poet William Wordsworth sensed, it imparts to the ear of faith 'authentic tidings of invisible things'. We have only to turn to such psalms as Psalm 18 and 19 to find that Scripture points to the signature of God in nature. He has never left himself without witness, and the apostle Paul can inform the citizens of Lystra that 'he did good and gave you from heaven rains and fruitful seasons, satisfying your hearts with food and gladness' (Acts 14:17). In all the kindly provision and plenty of the natural world, the hand of God can be discerned.

The Bible does not, however, sentimentalize the witness of nature, or convey the unrealistic impression that everything in its garden is invariably lovely. Nature has its cruel and ruthless aspect too, for sin has spoiled its primitive harmony. So the creation itself needs to be redeemed, along with mankind (Romans 8:20-21). Because of this, nature as such cannot lead all the way to God. It points in the right direction, but it is unable to bring us to the goal. 'I lift up my eyes to the hills. From whence does my help come?' (Psalm 121:1). Not from the hills, but from their Creator: 'My help comes from the LORD, who made heaven and earth' (verse 2). The pantheist worships nature as God. The Christian worships God (partly) through nature.

## The revelation of God in conscience

We have already made reference to conscience as a factor which points to the existence of God. We must consider it now as a means of general revelation. The English word is derived from a Latin verb meaning to know together. The Greek term in the New Testament is similar. It is used, for example, to describe what Ananias did in disposing of some property with his wife's connivance (Acts 5:2).

The word does not occur in the Old Testament at all. The operation of conscience is there ascribed to the 'heart' as being in a sense its equivalent. After David had disobeyed God by taking a census of the people, we are told that his 'heart smote him' (2 Samuel 24:10). In other words, he had an attack of conscience and knew he had done wrong. In further Old Testament passages the effects of an offended conscience are penetratingly delineated without actually resorting to a specific term to identify it (cf. Psalm 32:1–5; 51:1–9).

In the New Testament conscience is mentioned mainly in the writings of the apostle Paul. It is noteworthy that Jesus never used the word at all, although of course his teaching was calculated to heighten the moral awareness of his hearers. He made it clear that the inside as well as the outside of the cup must be kept clean (Matthew 23:26) and that sin begins in the heart and in the mind (Matthew 15:18–19; James 1:14–15).

The Bible teaches us that conscience is one of the means by which God reveals himself and makes known his will. What in the story of Pinnochio is graphically alluded to as 'the drummer in the heart' persistently beats out the message that man is accountable for what he does. But conscience is not to be regarded negatively as an early-warning system to avert moral disaster. More positively, it acts as an inner monitor to guide us along the right path and bring peace and satisfaction.

As in the case of nature, the role of conscience is to point beyond itself. While it can show the way, it is incapable of empowering the will to walk along it. Only when cleansed, sharpened and informed by the Holy Spirit does it become a fully effective instrument (Hebrews 9:13–14).

## The revelation of God in secular history

History is a link between the two aspects of revelation that we are examining. Secular history belongs to the sphere of God's general disclosure of himself to all, whereas sacred history (or salvation-history, as scholars tend to call it) is part of special revelation and must be treated within that category. God is not only at work in history through those who acknowledge him. He controls the entire sequence of events, and fulfils his purposes even by means of men and nations who are not conscious that they are his instruments.

Assyria is addressed in Isaiah's prophecy as the rod of the Lord's anger and the staff of his fury by means of which he chastises his own people (Isaiah 10:5). Cyrus the Great, founder of the Persian empire, by whose help Ezra was enabled to return to Jerusalem and restore it, is even referred to as the Lord's anointed – that is, one commissioned by him to further his plans (Isaiah 45:1). God says of Cyrus, 'He is my shepherd, and he shall fulfil all my purpose' (Isaiah 44:28). It is recognized in Scripture that human authority derives from God.

Kings and governors and magistrates only exercise their power because they are permitted to do so. 'The Most High rules the kingdom of men, and gives it to whom he will' (Daniel 4:25; cf. 5:21). That being so, any authority exercised by earthly potentates is merely delegated to them. Nebuchadnezzar, the Babylonian monarch who besieged the city of Jerusalem in the year 586 B.C. and carried off the Jews into exile, was nevertheless under God's control. The prophet Daniel addressed him as 'the king of kings, to whom the God of heaven has given the kingdom, the power, and the might, and the glory' (Daniel

2:37), and adds that he is the one in whose hands God has placed not only the citizens of his empire but even 'the beasts of the field, and the birds of the air', making him ruler over all (verse 38). We are told that it was the Lord himself who delivered Jehoaikim king of Judah into his hand when Jerusalem fell (Daniel 1:2).

That is why Jesus could tell Pontius Pilate to his face, 'You would have no power over me unless it had been given you from above' (John 19:11). 'Jesus is not thinking of Caesar as having invested Pilate with power,' explains one commentator here, 'but of God whose providence had allowed a man of Pilate's stamp to be placed in the procurator's office at this time.'

Within the wider sweep of secular history, however, God is working out his purpose in an even more explicit fashion. There is, so to speak, a history alongside history. It is the history of salvation. It leads to the sending of God's one and only Son into the world to make reconciliation possible. It is here that we move from God's general revelation of himself in nature, conscience and secular history to his special revelation in sacred history, in Scripture and in Christ.

## The revelation of God in sacred history

'You are a people holy to the LORD your God,' Moses told the Israelites as they travelled towards the land that had been promised to them; 'the LORD your God has chosen you to be a people for his own possession, out of all the peoples that are on the face of the earth' (Deuteronomy 7:6). God's plan to redeem all mankind involved the choice of a whole nation to be devoted to him and to represent him in the world. But again and again Israel proved to be disobedient and even rebellious. In the end they were disciplined by banishment from their country and sent off into exile in Babylon. Yet there was always a remnant who remained faithful, and it was through this nucleus that God proposed to bring his design to completion.

It was after the return to Jerusalem and the restoration of the nation Israel, that the expectation of a coming deliverer grew deeper and stronger. God showed his people that one day he would send them a king in the succession of David who would be their anointed ruler, or Messiah (Isaiah 11:1–3). Under his authority, Israel would be used by God to bring the light of salvation to all the races of the earth. 'It shall come to pass in the latter days that the mountain of the house of the LORD shall be established as the highest of the mountains, and shall be raised above the hills; and all the nations shall flow to it' (Isaiah 2:2; cf. 49:6).

Yet again, the people of Israel failed to rise to the occasion. In their self-absorbtion they were blind to what God was doing. When their Messiah appeared in the person of Jesus from Nazareth, they did not recognize him. 'He came to his own home,' says John, 'and his own people received him not' (John 1:11). Nevertheless, it was in Christ that God completed his plan to save. 'When the time had fully come, God sent forth his Son, born of woman, born under the law, to redeem those who were under the law, so that we might receive adoption as sons' (Galatians 4:4–5). This is what God was leading up to from the start as he took action on the stage of history. His final revelation of himself is in Christ the living Word. So Peter Taylor Forsyth could claim that 'the spinal cord of history is redemption'.

## The revelation of God in Christ

The writer to the Hebrews relates God's disclosure of himself in sacred history to his supreme manifestation in Christ. 'In many and various ways God spoke of old to our fathers by the prophets; but in these last days he has spoken to us by a Son, whom he appointed the heir of all things' (Hebrews 1:1–2). If we want to know who God is, we look first of all at Jesus. 'He reflects the glory of God and bears the very stamp of his nature' (verse 3). 'No one has ever seen God,' John explains, 'but God's only Son, he who is nearest to the Father's heart, he has made him known' (John 1:18, New English Bible). Who else could do so? This is so obvious, once it is known who Jesus is, that we do not need to speak at any length about it. Throughout this book it will be apparent that we see God best and most in Christ.

One of our Lord's followers, Philip from Bethsaida, once said to him: 'Lord, show us the Father, and we shall be satisfied' (John 14:8). Jesus must have sighed with sorrow that his men had still not cottoned on to what he had tried to tell them about himself. 'Have I been with you so long, and yet you do not know me, Philip? He who has seen me has seen the Father; how can you say, "Show us the Father"? Do you not believe that I am in the Father and the Father in me? The words that I say to you I do not speak on my own authority, but the Father who dwells in me does his works. Believe me that I am in the Father and the Father in me' (verses 9–11).

If, however, God has revealed himself fully and finally in the Lord Jesus Christ, how can we come to know him today? Jesus belongs to history: what about now? Jesus does indeed belong to history, but not only to the past. According to Scripture, he is 'the same yesterday and today and for ever' (Hebrews 13:8). He is the living Word, and as such we can meet him in a personal encounter still.

## The revelation of God in Scripture

In order that men may have the opportunity to be introduced to Christ as a present Saviour and Friend, God has made himself known also in the written word of the Bible. This too is part of his special revelation, although of course it is secondary to his disclosure in Christ. Scripture is a *witness* pointing throughout to Christ and the salvation he brings. Paul reminds Timothy that from childhood he was familiar 'with the sacred writings which are able to instruct you for salvation through faith in Christ Jesus' (2 Timothy 3:15).

Scripture is also a *record*, telling the story of redemption from the first. It traces the whole of sacred history from the creation to the cross and beyond to the empty tomb. Apart from the Bible, we would know nothing about God's master plan set out in Christ for the fullness of time, 'to unite all things in him, things in heaven and things on earth' (Ephesians 1:10).

Scripture, however, is more than a witness and a record. It is itself a *revelation*. God still makes himself known through its pages, as the Holy Spirit enables us to grasp the truth it contains. He speaks to us in unmistakably forthright and often disturbing terms. 'For the word of God is living and active, sharper than any two-edged sword, piercing to the division of soul and spirit, of joints and marrow, and discerning the thoughts and intentions of the heart' (Hebrews 4:12). What meets us in the Bible is not simply a dead chronicle, but a vital, penetrating, challenging, here-and-now revelation of God.

# 5

# THE GENERAL NAMES OF GOD

What kind of being is God? When he approaches us, as we look for him, whom do we meet? That is the most vital question of all in relation to God. As the Greek philosopher Aristotle recognized, the crucial issue is not whether there is a God but what kind of a God he is. We have seen how misleading, and even dangerous, wrong views of him can be. When we are introduced to him in his revelation of himself, what sort of a character does he bear?

The Bible teaches us about God mainly in two ways. It lets us know the names by which he has identified himself, and it indicates the attributes or qualities which belong to his nature. It is principally in these two directions that we discover what God is like, and a consideration of them will occupy us throughout the rest of the book. In this chapter and the next, we shall be dealing with the general and particular names of God.

## The name of God

The Bible often speaks about the name of God in the singular. The third commandment runs: 'You shall not take the name of the LORD your God in vain; for the LORD will not hold him guiltless who takes his name in vain' (Exodus 20:7). 'O LORD, our Lord,' exclaims the psalmist, 'how majestic is thy name in all the earth!' (Psalm 8:1). And again, 'those who know thy name put their trust in thee, for thou, O LORD, hast not forsaken those who seek thee' (Psalm 9:10). According to the writer of Proverbs (18:10), 'The name of the LORD is a strong tower;

the righteous man runs into it and is safe' – a reference to the plight of a refugee escaping from hostile pursuers and his relief in finding a place to hide.

In these, and many other instances which could be quoted from the Old Testament Scriptures, the name of God stands for his manifestation of himself. In Hebrew thought, a name is not just a label. It is a description. The name of God is more than a copper-plate inscription on a visiting card. It is his own disclosure of who he is. The name is the person revealed.

It is, moreover, the person as actually and actively present. The contest on Carmel was a trial of names. 'You call on the name of your god,' Elijah told the prophets of Baal, 'and I will call on the name of the LORD; and the God who answers by fire, he is God' (1 Kings 18:24). It was not simply a matter of invoking a name as such. The one who carried the name was being challenged to prove himself by doing something. The name of God, then, in biblical terms, is himself in his essential character as expressed by his personal presence and action. So far from being abstract and theoretical, as might perhaps be supposed, it is concrete and practical in its implications.

## Elohim

The first of God's general names to appear in Scripture is *Elohim*. It is used in the opening verse of Genesis – 'In the beginning God created the heavens and the earth' (Genesis 1:1), and recurs throughout the creation story down to Genesis 2:3. It is employed with great frequency in the Old Testament and is second only to the covenant name of God, which is Yahweh. It is applied not only to the one true God of Israel, but also to pagan deities and monarchs (Exodus 18:11; 1 Samuel 4:8; 2 Kings 18:23), to angels (Job 1:6; 2:1; 38:7) and to magistrates (Exodus 19:7; 22:28).

It is probably connected with El, meaning mighty or strong, and may thus be taken to represent God as the putter-forth of energy. However, some scholars link it with another Hebrew root which has to do with being timid or shy, in which case the name would suggest the trembling awe men feel in the presence of the highest. Either interpretation is in line with what we learn about God elsewhere in Scripture. He is all-powerful and is therefore to be revered.

It is noteworthy that Elohim is plural and yet, when used of God, is usually followed by a singular verb. For example, in Genesis 1:26 we read: 'Then God [Elohim] said [singular], "Let us make man in our image, after our likeness."' This remarkable combination of singular and plural forms foreshadows the later revelation of the New Testament that within the unity of the Godhead three persons cohere. Even if we regard Elohim as a collective noun, its bearing on the doctrine of the Trinity is not lost.

The plural Elohim when used of God in the Old Testament clearly carries a singular meaning. Joshua warned the people, 'You cannot serve the LORD; for he is [singular] a holy God [Elohim, plural]; he is [singular] a jealous God [Elohim, plural]; he will not forgive your transgressions or your sins' (Joshua 24:19). A recurring phrase 'the LORD is [singular] God [Elohim, plural]' underlines the fact that Elohim is no doubt a plural of divine majesty (Deuteronomy 4:35, 39; 1 Kings 8:60; 18:39; Isaiah 45:18). The Queen begins her official speeches before Parliament, or elsewhere, with 'we' not 'I'. But, as we have already pointed out, in the case of Elohim the usage is not merely conventional. It reflects the reality of God's nature.

Sometimes Elohim is preceded by the definite article 'the' and thus unambiguously refers to the one true God, for such a construction is never found when heathen deities are involved. Only God is the Elohim – the mighty One or the One to be feared – but the word can have the same meaning without the prefix (cf. 1 Kings 18:21, 37; Genesis 1:1; 9:27; Amos 4:11). These distinctions, however, cannot easily be conveyed in an English translation. It is interesting, moreover, that both Elohim (plural) and El (singular) occur together in Nehemiah 9:32 – 'Now therefore, our God [Elohim, plural], the great and mighty and terrible God [El, singular], who keepest covenant and steadfast love, let not all the hardship seem little to thee that has come upon us.' All this confirms that even in the Old Testament the germ of a trinitarian understanding of God's nature begins to present itself.

In the Old Testament Scriptures, the singular El, however, is often combined with an appropriate adjective to produce a double-barrelled name of God which reveals a particular aspect of his nature. These derivations of El are unusually instructive. We must look at them next.

## El Elyon

The first in order of appearance is *El Elyon*, or God Most High. Melchizedek, that enigmatic figure who resembles the Son of God who came in the flesh (Hebrews 7:3), is introduced as 'priest of God Most High' (Genesis 14:18). We are told that he blessed Abraham, through whom all nations were in turn to be blessed, saying: 'Blessed be Abram by God Most High, maker of heaven and earth; and blessed be God Most High, who has delivered your enemies into your hand!' (verses 19–20). In his reply, Abraham repeated the designation (verse 22). The name is found again precisely in this form in Psalm 78:35 – 'the Most High God their redeemer'.

The prophecy of Balaam in the presence of Balak, king of Moab, also looked forward to the advent of Christ, and is introduced as 'the oracle of him who hears the words of God, and knows the knowledge of the Most High' (Numbers 24:16). The taunt against the king of Babylon recorded by Isaiah is thought to be directed also against Satan, as the prince of darkness, who was once Lucifer, the bearer of light. He said in his arrogant heart, 'I will ascend above the heights of the clouds, I will make myself like the Most High' (Isaiah 14:14). Instead, he was 'brought down to Sheol, to the depths of the Pit' (verse 15). In both these instances, Elyon (without El) is nevertheless plainly a divine title.

Elyon is derived from a root word meaning to go up. It refers to God's exaltation and supremacy. He is the One who is far above all. He is in absolute control of heaven and earth. He is the 'King of kings and Lord of lords' (1 Timothy 6:15). Nothing and no one is higher than God. Indeed, compared with his unimaginable greatness, any brief and puny authority man may imagine he possesses shrinks into a vacuum. God alone is pre-eminent and so God alone is to be glorified.

This sense of the divine exaltation is carried over into the New Testament and finds expression in passages of praise like the doxology already quoted from 1 Timothy (6:15–16), where God is hailed as 'the blessed and only Sovereign ... who alone has immortality and dwells in unapproachable light, whom no man has ever seen or can see. To him be honour and eternal dominion. Amen.'

## El Shaddai

*El Shaddai* is a title first used by God in an encounter with Abraham. When Abraham was ninety-nine years of age, we learn that the Lord appeared to him and said, 'I am God Almighty [El Shaddai]; walk before me, and be blameless' (Genesis 17:1). The name recurs in the narratives relating to the patriarch Jacob (Genesis 28:3; 35:11; 43:14; 48:3; 49:25), and in Exodus 6:3, where God reminds Moses that he appeared to Abraham, to Isaac and to Jacob as God Almighty (El Shaddai). In many other Old Testament passages, Shaddai occurs without the prefix El, but always with clear reference to God. The designation is particularly common in the book of Job.

The translation 'Almighty' assumes that the original Hebrew root signifies power. In support of this claim, it is argued that in Genesis 49:24–25, El Shaddai is used in parallel with 'the Mighty One of Jacob', and that the play on words in Isaiah 13:6 and Joel 1:15 – 'destruction from the Almighty' – confirms this interpretation. Others think that the verb means to treat with violence, which would rather imply that God is the destroyer of those who oppose him, and indeed this would seem to be the point of the pun in the passages from Isaiah and Joel referred to above.

More recently a case has been made out for interpreting El

Shaddai as 'the God of the mountain', with reference to 'the Rock of Israel' in Genesis 49:24. This would preserve the idea of God's power and connect it with that of protection. The traditional Jewish understanding of the title still retains its attractiveness, however, with its emphasis on the divine sufficiency. El Shaddai is 'the enough God', as one commentator put it, who has ample resources to meet our every need.

## El Olam

*El Olam*, the Everlasting God, is another of the titles disclosed to Abraham. After Abraham and Abimelech had made a covenant at Beersheba, the former planted a tamarisk tree there which is said to have survived to this day. He then 'called there on the name of the LORD, the Everlasting God' (Genesis 21:33). 'Have you not known? Have you not heard?' enquired the prophet Isaiah; 'The LORD is the everlasting God [El Olam], the Creator of the ends of the earth. He does not faint or grow weary' (Isaiah 40:28). It is because of this that he can strengthen and sustain his people (cf. verses 29–31).

El Olam is not only the eternal, but also the one who is always adaptable. He adjusts himself to the changing situation of his children. There is no predicament in which we may find ourselves which takes him by surprise. God sees the end from the beginning and anticipates every development, however unexpected it may be to us. In each generation his people prove him to be the one who enables them to cope with whatever may arise. It is a suitable name to be associated with a formal treaty which was regarded as binding in perpetuity. 'His steadfast [or covenant] love endures for ever, and his faithfulness to all generations' (Psalm 100:5; cf. 103:17).

## El Roi

*El Roi*, the God of Seeing, is a title used by Hagar, Sarah's maid, when the Lord graciously made himself known to her in the desert after she had conceived her son Ishmael. 'Thou art a God of seeing [El Roi],' she exclaimed; 'Have I really seen God and remained alive after seeing him?' (Genesis 16:13). And so the spring of water where the angel of the Lord found her was called Beer-lahai-roi, the well of the living one, who sees (verse 14). God allows himself to be seen and at the same time sees everything. There is nothing concealed from him. (The LORD looks down from heaven, he sees all the sons of men; from where he sits enthroned he looks forth on all the inhabitants of the earth, he who fashions the hearts of them all, and observes all their deeds' (Psalm 33:13–15).

The same idea recurs in the letter to the Hebrews where, after referring to the penetrative effect of God's word, the author says concerning the Lord that 'before him no creature is hidden, but all are open and laid bare to the eyes of him with whom we have to do' (Hebrews 4:13). After the Fall, Adam and Eve tried to hide themselves from God's scrutiny, but found it impossible to do so (Genesis 3). The psalmist realized that there is no place where a man can escape from the eyes of the God who sees (Psalm 139:7–12). We cannot do anything behind God's back as it were. He is always there to see. To the disobedient, like Jonah, God's presence is a judgement. To the outcast, like Hagar, it is an offer of grace.

Other compounds of El are less important, although each of them has something further to reveal about the character of God. He is *El Rechum*, the God of Compassion (Deuteronomy 4:31), *El Nose'*, the Forgiving God (Psalm 99:8), *El Channum*, the Gracious God (Nehemiah 9:31), *El Kanna*, the Jealous God (Exodus 20:5) and *El-Elohe-Israel*, God the God of Israel.

## Adonai

Another general name for God which demands our attention before we close our survey is *Adonai*, Lord. Like Elohim, this is a plural form. The singular, *adon*, means in the first place a judge, and then master or chief. It is used of God without a definite article, only in Psalm 114:7 – 'Tremble, O earth, at the presence of [the] LORD.' As 'the *Adon*' it occurs in Malachi

3:1 – 'the Lord whom you seek will suddenly come to his temple' – and more often in conjunction with other divine names (Exodus 23:17; 34:23; Isaiah 1:24; 3:1). The plural Adonai is much more frequent. It is found first in Genesis 15:2 when Abraham addresses Yahweh as 'Lord [Adonai] GOD [Yahweh]'. The same expression recurs in verse 8.

This was the name for God which was most familiar to the Jews. They used it as a substitute for Yahweh, which was considered too holy actually to pronounce. It means that God is the ruling Lord. He is the one who demands unwavering obedience. The term is employed at the human level to denote the relationship between a king and his subjects, a husband and his wife, and a master and his slaves. As our King, God demands homage (cf. Psalm 45:11). As a husband, he seeks not only submissiveness, but love in return for love (Isaiah 54:5–8). As a master, he requires respect and unquestioning obedience (Malachi 3:17–18). To recognize God as Adonai is to forsake every lesser allegiance. As Jesus taught, we cannot serve two masters (Matthew 6:24). We must choose between God and wealth. There is no room for both. We need to confess in the language of Isaiah: 'O LORD our God, other lords besides thee have ruled over us, but thy name alone we acknowledge' (Isaiah 26:13).

# 6

# THE COVENANT NAME OF GOD

The special or covenant name of God in Hebrew is *Yahweh*. It is by far the most often used in the Old Testament, and is indeed the controlling designation of the deity. Unlike Elohim, El and even on occasion Adonai, it is never under any circumstances applied to false gods nor does it have a secular connotation. It is the name for God above all others.

It is usually translated as 'Lord' but, in order to avoid confusion with Adonai, is conveniently printed in capitals in most English Bibles. (The Jerusalem Bible uses 'Yahweh'.) Lord stands for Adonai and LORD for Yahweh. Similarly, Elohim appears as God, but Yahweh as GOD. It is helpful when studying the Old Testament to keep an eye open for distinctions. In the New Testament they disappear for, following the Septuagint (a Greek translation of the Old Testament), Adonai is substituted for Yahweh and rendered uniformly as *Kyrios* or Lord.

In a few instances in the Authorized Version of the Bible Yahweh is not rendered by LORD but transliterated as 'Jehovah' (Exodus 6:3; Psalm 83:18, Isaiah 12:2; 26:4). The reason why Yahweh (and thus Jehovah) appears in the form with which we are now familiar is particularly interesting. As we have seen, the Jews regarded the covenant name of God as too sacred to utter. Instead, the four consonants YHWH – known technically as the tetragrammaton (four letters) – were supplied with the vowels of Adonai to produce 'Yahweh' or 'Jehovah'. The shorter variation 'Jah' also occurs (Psalm 68:4).

In the strictest sense, as G. T. Manley argued, Yahweh is the only personal name of God. Wherever in Genesis the

Hebrew word for 'name' is linked with the divine being, Yahweh is used. Whenever the patriarchs erected an altar they 'called on the name of the LORD [Yahweh]' (Genesis 12:8; 13:4; 26:25). Yahweh is thus to be regarded as a proper noun, introducing God as a person and relating him to other human persons. 'It brings God near to man,' Manley proceeds to explain, 'and he speaks to the patriarchs as one friend to another.' It is not accidental that Yahweh is the name for God which dominates the second account of creation in Genesis (2:4–25), focusing as it does on the origins of man.

## Derivation

The name Yahweh is derived from the Hebrew verb to be. That is made clear in Exodus 3:13–15, where Moses dared to ask the God who had appeared to him at the burning bush by what new name he might now be known, as he was about to deliver his children from oppression in Egypt. 'God said to Moses, "I AM WHO I AM." And he said, "Say this to the people of Israel, 'I AM has sent me to you'"' (Exodus 3:14). The next verse makes it clear that 'I AM WHO I AM' is an amplification of 'Yahweh': 'Say this to the people of Israel, "the LORD [Yahweh], the God of your fathers, the God of Abraham, the God of Isaac, and the God of Jacob, has sent me to you": this is my name for ever, and thus I am to be remembered throughout all generations' (verse 15).

Already there has been a clue in verse 12. God has assured Moses, 'I will be with you.' Now in verse 14 he says, 'I AM WHO I AM.' The tense is indefinite. It may combine past, present and future – I was, I am, I shall be. Some regard the expression as suggesting that God is the self-existent one – the one who exists by himself independently of all other beings. This, however, sounds more like Greek than Hebrew thought, and in any case, the experts assure us that the syntax of the sentence rules out this possibility. Others think that the divine name has to do with God's activity in creation, as the one who causes to be.

It seems more likely that the name is to be taken in close conjunction with what goes before and follows after, and contains an assurance of God's presence: 'I was with you, I am with you, I will be with you.' To this may be added the comment of Professor A. B. Davidson:

> What he will be is left unexpressed – he will be to his people all that they need (the element of relationship is prominent in the conception) – helper, comforter, deliverer.

In other words, in revealing his personal name in this fashion, God was supplying his children with a blank cheque and inviting them to fill it in to any amount in any currency. It represents his guarantee to keep all his promises, and be to those who trust in him all that he has said he would be. The apostle Paul was simply drawing out all that this incomparable name implies when he assured the Christians in Philippi: 'My God will supply every need of yours according to his riches in glory in Christ Jesus' (Philippians 4:19).

## The covenant

It is in the covenant he has entered into with his chosen people that God has pledged himself to be their provider. Hence Yahweh is specifically the covenant name of God. It is the name used to ratify the agreement and it also expresses the benefits which ensue. 'Know therefore that the LORD [Yahweh] your God is God, the faithful God who keeps covenant and steadfast love with those who love him and keep his commandments, to a thousand generations' (Deuteronomy 7:9).

What was true of the foundation covenant, which was spelled out in its developed form in the book of Deuteronomy, is equally so of the new, or rather renewed covenant set out in Jeremiah 31:31–34. The prophecy confirms Jeremiah's assurance of a future for the nation but links it with the earlier covenant and the name Yahweh. 'This is the covenant which I will make with the house of Israel after those days, says the LORD [Yahweh]: I will put my law within them, and I will write it upon their hearts; and I will be their God, and they shall be my people' (Jeremiah 31:33).

The essence of the covenant relationship is that God has undertaken to provide a means by which sinful man might be reconciled to himself. This, of course, was only fulfilled in Christ who was sent to be the atoning sacrifice through which the damage done by sin was repaired (1 John 4:10). God's new covenant was sealed by the redemptive death of Christ (Hebrews 9:15–18), and it is significant that the Son should bear the name of *Jesus*, or *Yahweh saves* (cf. Matthew 1:21).

From Genesis 2:4 onwards Yahweh as the personal name of God remains constant throughout the Scriptures of the Old Testament. Elohim also continues as the more general name. Sometimes the two are used together – the LORD God (Yahweh Elohim). In addition to this, the covenant name Yahweh is prefixed to a series of titles which provide further descriptions of God's character. These compounds of Yahweh or Jehovah correspond to the redemptive experiences of his people. Through them we come to know more specifically who God is and what he is able to do for and through his people. We must briefly glance at eight such titles.

1. *Jehovah-Tsidkenu, the Lord our Righteousness.* This designation is used only by Jeremiah, and in two senses. It is applied to the coming Messiah, the 'righteous Branch of David', who will 'reign as king' (Jeremiah 23:5). 'In his days Judah will be saved, and Israel will dwell securely. And this is the name by which he will be called: "The LORD [Yahweh] is our righteousness"' (Jeremiah 23:6). In the second reference (Jeremiah 33:16), the same title is bestowed on the city of Jerusalem, as being the seat of Messiah's rule.

If we are to enjoy communion with God, the first requirement is righteousness. This, of course, is something we can never produce ourselves, for it is not in us to do so. If ever we are to gain access to God, and acceptance with him, then a righteousness other than our own will have to be provided for us.

This, in fact, is exactly what God has supplied in Christ.

He himself will be the Lord our Righteousness. As we have seen
from its occurrence in Jeremiah, this title relates to the Messiah.
It points to Christ whom God made to be 'our righteousness'
(1 Corinthians 1:30). 'For our sake he made him to be sin who
knew no sin, so that in him we might become the righteousness
of God' (2 Corinthians 5:21).

2. *Jehovah-Mekaddischem, the Lord our Sanctifier*. This is
probably the least familiar of these successive titles. Unlike the
others, it is not transliterated, either in the text or in the margin.
Yet it is one of the most meaningful of all and is closely
connected with Jehovah-Tsidkenu. It is found initially in
Exodus 31:12–13 in the context of sabbath observance. 'And
the LORD [Yahweh] said to Moses, "Say to the people of Israel,
'You shall keep my sabbaths, for this is a sign between me and
you throughout your generations, that you may know that I,
the LORD [Yahweh], sanctify you.'"' One day in seven was to
be set apart from the rest and reserved for God. Separation
is the heart of sanctification. Those who belong to God are set
apart for him. 'Consecrate yourselves therefore, and be holy;
for I am the LORD [Yahweh] your God. Keep my statutes, and
do them; I am the LORD [Yahweh] who sanctify you' (Leviticus
20:7–8; cf. 21:8, 15, 23; 22:9, 16, 32).

Sanctification, then, is at once God's own work in us and
yet something we must seek by offering ourselves to him. It
is made possible in Christ, who is not only our redemption and
righteousness, but our sanctification as well (1 Corinthians 1:30).

3. *Jehovah-Jireh, the Lord Will Provide*. After Abraham had
sacrificed the ram that God had made available in place of his
son Isaac, we read that he called the name of the place on Mount
Moriah 'The LORD [Yahweh] will provide' (Genesis 22:14). By
the time the event was recorded, the saying had evidently passed
into a proverb.

As the footnote in the Revised Standard Version indicates,
the title could also be translated as 'The LORD [Yahweh] will
see', which might also seem to fit the circumstances. Or again,

the meaning may be 'Yahweh will be seen, or let himself be seen'. There is no real discrepancy, however, since the Hebrew word involved carries this appropriate double allusion to vision and provision. The Lord sees each situation and reveals himself in it by supplying what man lacks. The Lord, who is our Righteousness and our Sanctifier, also offers his Son as the Lamb of God who takes away the sin of the world (John 1:29).

4. *Jehovah-Shalom, the Lord our Peace*. This is the name Gideon gave to the altar he set up in Ophrah, when the angel of Yahweh assured him that Israel would be delivered from the marauding Midianites. He himself was concerned for his life, since he had seen the angel face to face. 'But the LORD [Yahweh] said to him, "Peace be to you; do not fear, you shall not die." Then Gideon built an altar there to the LORD [Yahweh], and called it, The LORD [Yahweh] is peace' (Judges 6:23–24).

Through his covenant, God not only brings his people relief from the attacks of their enemies but, even more importantly, peace with himself. 'Thou dost keep him in perfect peace, whose mind is stayed on thee, because he trusts in thee' (Isaiah 26:3). Peace of heart, mind and conscience flow from the reconciliation which Christ died to achieve on our behalf. When by faith we are brought into a right relationship with God, then we have peace with him through our Lord Jesus Christ (Romans 5:1).

5. *Jehovah-Nissi, the Lord our Banner*. After God had given the Israelites a desert victory over the Amalekites at Rephidim, Moses constructed an altar on the spot and called it 'The LORD [Yahweh] is my banner, saying, "A hand upon the banner of the LORD [Yahweh]!"' (Exodus 17:15–16). The title Jehovah-Nissi occurs here only, but the idea behind it, namely that God is the giver of victory and the one around whom his people rally, is common (e.g. Psalm 60:4; Isaiah 62:10; Jeremiah 4:21).

In the New Testament the warfare in which God's soldiers engage is seen to be spiritual as we fight the good fight of faith (2 Timothy 4:7). There is no doubt, however, about the outcome of the conflict. Victory is secure, for 'we are more than conquerors through him who loved us' (Romans 8:37).

6. *Jehovah-Rapha, the Lord our Healer*. At Marah, where bitter water was sweetened by divine intervention, we are told that Yahweh himself gave his people an undertaking that if they obeyed him then he would not visit them with any of the diseases with which he had afflicted the Egyptians, 'for I am the LORD [Yahweh] your healer' (Exodus 15:26). Moses was the first in Scripture to invoke the name of God for physical healing, when Miriam was smitten with leprosy (Numbers 12:13). Henceforward the Lord could be praised as the one who heals all our diseases (Psalm 103:3). Whenever recovery takes place, it comes from him.

A deeper truth, however, is taught by this title. Physical healing is not the greatest miracle. God can restore the sin-sick soul. The primary benefit for which the LORD's name is praised in Psalm 103 is not the curing of illness but the forgiveness of iniquity. 'If we confess our sins, he is faithful and just, and will forgive our sins and cleanse us from all unrighteousness' (1 John 1:9).

7. *Jehovah-Rohi, the Lord our Shepherd*. 'The LORD [Yahweh] is my shepherd, I shall not want' (Psalm 23:1). This motif is common in the Psalter (cf. Psalm 80:1; 95:7; 100:3). Isaiah comforts the Jews in exile with the assurance that the Lord God (Adonai Yahweh) 'will feed his flock like a shepherd' and take them back to their own land (Isaiah 40:11). The fullest pastoral picture of all is to be found in the prophecy of Ezekiel – 'I myself will be the shepherd of my sheep' (Ezekiel 34:15; cf. verses 11–16).

It is no coincidence that Jesus, using the divine name 'I am', described himself as the Good Shepherd who lays down his life for the sheep (John 10:11). It was in the person of his Son that God showed himself to be Jehovah-Rohi indeed.

8. *Jehovah-Shammah, the Lord is There*. This title appears only in Ezekiel 48:35, where it rounds off the entire prophecy. The

vision of a reinstated and enhanced Jerusalem at the end of the age, when the Messiah returns, leads to this disclosure: 'And the name of the city henceforth shall be, The LORD [Yahweh] is there.' In judgement 'the glory of the LORD [Yahweh] went up from the midst of the city' (Ezekiel 11:23) at the time of its destruction. In chapter 43 we are shown how once again 'the glory of the LORD [Yahweh] filled the temple' (verse 5) in the prophet's vision of restoration.

Here is God's ultimate goal for his chosen people – that they should no longer rebel and disobey, but dwell in the place he has appointed for them and prove his presence to be a reality. The New Testament presents an even more sublime description of 'the holy city, new Jerusalem, coming down out of heaven from God, prepared as a bride adorned for her husband' (Revelation 21:2). A great voice was heard from the throne saying, 'Behold, the dwelling of God is with men. He will dwell with them, and they shall be his people, and God himself will be with them' (Revelation 21:3). In the final realization of God's purpose for his people, and indeed for the whole earth, it will be evident beyond any disputing the 'the LORD [Yahweh] is there.'

## Yahweh Sabaoth – the Lord of Hosts

In a rather different category from the personal names which we have listed is the divine title Yahweh Sabaoth, the Lord of hosts. This is a later construction not found in the Pentateuch (the first five books of the Bible). It is mentioned in connection with the shrine at Shiloh, where the sons of Eli ministered as priests (1 Samuel 1:3). It became a battle-cry after David had challenged Goliath 'in the name of the LORD [Yahweh] of hosts, the God of the armies of Israel' (1 Samuel 17:45). The one who commands all the heavenly powers is well able to defend and deliver his people. 'The LORD [Yahweh] of hosts is with us' (Psalm 46:7, 11) is no empty boast, but voices the exultation of those who know that God is on their side if they are on his.

# 7

# THE FATHERHOOD OF GOD

In our survey so far, and especially in considering the names of God, we have concentrated very largely on the Scriptures of the Old Testament. It is here that we first learn about God in his essential being and in the character he bears. The New Testament builds on this foundation, confirming and expanding what has already been disclosed. It goes on to show that within the unity of the Godhead three persons are encountered – Father, Son, and Holy Spirit. The distinctively Christian doctrine of God is trinitarian in shape.

Even apart from this revelation, however, the New Testament completes and crowns the teaching of the Old by highlighting the name of Father. There is no more suitable way of describing God than this. The climax of the divine self-disclosure is reached when the Almighty allows himself to be approached as the Father of his children. Here is the Christian view of God in a nutshell. After we have rehearsed the various names for him to be discovered in Scripture, Father is the best and most comprehensive of all.

## The teaching of Jesus

It was Jesus, of course, who taught his disciples to say 'Our Father' (Matthew 6:9). They had asked him how they should draw near to God in prayer, and this was the mode of address he encouraged them to use. Should we ever be invited to meet some very important person – a member of the royal family, a leading statesman, or a peer of the realm – it would prove necessary to know the precise title by which such a dignitary ought to be approached. How infinitely more essential it is to find the correct formula when entering the presence of the One who is the King of kings and Lord of lords! Yet Jesus says we need not bother about using some high-sounding title. We can simply call God Father. That is not to assume a familiarity which could breed irreverence. It is to avail ourselves of an intimacy which God himself has made possible, through what he has done for us in making us his children by adoption and grace.

## Abba

The word Jesus used to address God as Father is Abba. That is Aramaic – the Palestinian language Jesus himself spoke. Abba is simple to pronounce, like its English equivalent, Daddy. Even a baby could manage to say it. Indeed it was invariably the first word to fall from the lips of Jewish children. No doubt Jesus had used it when he looked up into Joseph's face. According to the Talmud – a collection of sayings from the rabbis – 'When a child experiences the taste of wheat (that is, after it has been weaned and can take solid food) it learns to say Abba and Imma.' Abba and Imma are baby words for Daddy and Mummy.

But Abba was something more than simply a babbling sound. Although it began as that, it was not abandoned when children grew up. It remained the family name for father. Sons and daughters continued to employ it even when they had become parents themselves, as we know from the Dead Sea Scrolls. Only on formal occasions would a father be addressed as sir. In one of the tales Jesus told, the second of two sons invited to work in his father's vineyard was trying to impress by his exaggerated politeness when he responded, 'I go, sir,' (Matthew 21:30). In the more familiar parable of the two sons, the prodigal evidently used this Aramaic term Abba (Luke 15:12, 18, 21).

Because it was such a cosy and domestic word, no Jew would ever have dreamed of applying it to God. Many hundreds of

Jewish prayers, both corporate and personal, have been preserved but, as Professor Joachim Jeremias has shown, nowhere is that kind of invocation ever to be found. It would have been considered far too irreverent to employ such a familiar term as Abba with reference to God. Yet this is just what Jesus did.

We are told this explicitly in the account of the betrayal of Jesus recorded by Mark. In Gethsemane Jesus went aside in order to pray that, if it were possible, the hour of testing might be avoided. 'And he said, "Abba, Father, all things are possible to thee; remove this cup from me; yet not what I will, but what thou wilt"' (Mark 14:36). Although this is the only place in the gospels where this Aramaic word is actually transcribed, the scholars tell us that the way in which the Greek for 'my Father' or simply 'Father' is used elsewhere indicates that Jesus habitually resorted to it. The language in the garden, under the deepest emotional stress, reflected the practice of a lifetime. Indeed, there is only one prayer of Jesus where the preface 'My Father' is lacking. Significantly, it is the cry from the cross as he bore the separation of our sins: 'My God, my God, why hast thou forsaken me?' (Mark 15:34; cf. Psalm 22:1).

## The practice of Christians

It is sufficiently remarkable and indeed revolutionary that Jesus himself should have ventured to call God Father. What is even more astounding is that he allowed and even advised his disciples to do the same (cf. Matthew 6:9). That this developed into a regular pattern in the primitive Christian community is reflected in two passages from Paul's correspondence. Writing to the Romans, the apostle explains: 'When we cry, "Abba! Father!" it is the Spirit himself bearing witness with our spirit that we are children of God' (Romans 8:15–16). Similarly he reminds the Galatians: 'And because you are sons, God has sent the Spirit of his Son into our hearts, crying, "Abba! Father!"' (Galatians 4:6). As Professor Jeremias points out, this applies both to churches missioned by Paul, like those in Galatia, and

to those like Rome which were founded by others. He thinks
that there can be no doubt at all that this early Christian
exclamation is an echo of Christ's own praying.

## The Old Testament

Although it is in the New Testament, and above all in the teaching of Jesus himself, that the distinctively Christian revelation of
God as Father is to be found, it must not therefore be assumed
that there is no hint at all of such an idea in the Old Testament.
This is certainly not the case. Although by no means prominent,
the fatherhood of God is not entirely absent either. But it is
not interpreted in a personal fashion. God is seen rather as the
Father of the nation Israel as a whole.

## Father of the nation

Moses was instructed to inform Pharaoh, 'Thus says the LORD,
Israel is my first-born son, and I say to you, "Let my son go
that he may serve me"' (Exodus 4:22–23). 'When Israel was
a child, I loved him, and out of Egypt I called my son'; so
the Lord movingly reminded his people in Hosea 11:1. Hence
Moses could rebuke the disobedient Israelites because they had
proved to be unworthy of their heritage as his children
(Deuteronomy 32:5). 'Do you thus requite the LORD, you foolish
and senseless people? Is not he your father, who created you,
who made you and established you?' (verse 6).

God, then, is regarded as the founder and originator of the
nation. He is in this sense 'a father to Israel' (Jeremiah 31:9).
Hence his people can confess: 'For thou art our Father ... thou,
O LORD, art our Father, our Redeemer from of old is thy name'
(Isaiah 63:16). He is the one who brought deliverance from
oppression in Egypt and established his people in the land he
had promised for them. This relationship was sealed by the
covenant into which God had entered with his children.

## Creator of the race

In the Old Testament, however, God is seen not only as the
Father of the nation but also as the Creator of the race. That
has already been implied in the passage from Deuteronomy
(32:6), quoted above, where clearly God is envisaged not simply
as the architect of the community but as the giver of life. That
is made even more explicit in Isaiah 64:8 – 'Yet, O LORD, thou
art our Father; we are the clay, and thou art our potter; we
are all the work of thy hand.' Hence Malachi can ask: 'Have
we not all one father? Has not one God created us?' (Malachi
2:10).

God is also regarded as Father in the sense that he cares for
what he has created. Despite the repeated ingratitude of his
people, he continues to treat them with loving concern and to
long for their response. 'And I thought you would call me, My
Father, and would not turn from following me' (Jeremiah 3:19).
The tenderness and compassion of God's loving heart is perhaps
nowhere more movingly expressed than in the words of the
psalmist: 'As a father pities his children, so the LORD pities
those who fear him. For he knows our frame; he remembers
that we are dust' (Psalm 103:13–14).

What, then, was anticipated here and there in the scriptures
of the Old Testament – where God is only spoken of as Father
fourteen times altogether – becomes the central feature of the
Christian revelation. 'A religion may call God by several names,'
according to James Moffatt, 'but there are titles for God without
which it would not be itself, and for Christianity the supreme
title is that of Father.'

## Personal relationship

In the New Testament the name Father is employed in a new
and personal sense. Although the individual Israelite recognized
that Yahweh was the Father of the chosen race (cf. John 8:41),
he was not in the habit of regarding God as his Father in any
one-to-one relationship. It was the distinctive contribution of

Jesus to insist that God is our Father not simply in a collective but in a personal sense. This was uniquely the case as far as his own sonship was concerned. Jesus did not address God as 'Our Father', as he had taught his followers to do. With him it was always 'My Father'. After his resurrection he told Mary, 'Go to my brethren and say to them, I am ascending to my Father and your Father, to my God and your God' (John 20:17). Two quite different relationships are involved. As the eternal Son, begotten before all time, the Lord Jesus stood in a singular relationship to the Father. No one else is *the* Son of God.

But this unique sonship of Christ is nevertheless the ground of ours as Christian believers. It is because he could say 'My Father' that we can pray 'Our Father'. That is the Lord's Prayer indeed – the prayer the Lord taught his disciples and the prayer which it is only possible to offer because of who the Lord is and what he has done for us. Thus the person of Christ is crucial to his teaching about the Fatherhood of God. It is not only what he said that counts: what matters is that he alone had the right to say it as the only-begotten Son of God. Who else knows better about the Father than the Son? That is why we pay special attention to what he has to tell us on this matter. There are twice as many references to God as Father in the gospels as elsewhere in the New Testament, including over one hundred in John alone.

## The distinctive name

In the two preceding chapters we examined the various names for God to be found in the Old Testament, many of which are corroborated by the New. For Christians the number one name for God is Father. It is in the New Testament – and most of all in the sayings of Jesus – that we are introduced to it. It is not that the fatherhood of God is a plus to be added to everything learnt about God from the Old Testament. 'Father' is not just one more name to be attached to the list as a postscript or even as the most significant of all. Fatherhood is rather the central, dominating idea in whose revealing light all the other names of God must be read and interpreted. It is, moreover, extended in its scope beyond the restricted confines of the nation Israel to include those of every race who recognize the lordship of Christ. It is not, of course, assumed that any are naturally children of the Father, for no one can inherit such a privilege by virtue of birth. But the possibility of becoming the Father's children by the new birth that the Spirit brings about is now available to all.

The Jews could no longer press the claims of their physical descent. When they protested, 'We have one Father, even God' (John 8:41), Jesus replied, 'If God were your Father, you would love me, for I proceeded and came forth from God' (verse 42). Neither reliance on impeccable ancestry ('Abraham is our father' verse 39) nor on orthodox doctrine ('we have one Father, even God' verse 41) will do. The only thing that matters now is to recognize that Jesus is the way: no one comes to the Father except by him (John 14:6). All others have another father – the devil (John 8:44). Those who would know God as Father must first acknowledge his Son as Saviour and Lord (Matthew 11:27; Luke 10:22).

It is a striking and relevant fact that Jesus never spoke to the crowds about the fatherhood of God. He only talked in private to his disciples along such lines, and even then with increasing intensity after Peter had confessed him as 'the Christ, the Son of the living God' (Matthew 16:16) at Caesarea Philippi. The privilege of addressing and experiencing God as Father belongs exclusively to those who have received new life through the Son (John 1:12).

What in fact did Jesus intend us to understand when he taught that God is Father? The name lets us look into the very heart of the Almighty. To be a father is to delight in giving. That is true even on the human level. A father who is worthy of the name puts himself out to provide what his child requires. If his son wanted a loaf of bread, no father would try to fob him off with a stone, said Jesus; nor if he fancied a fish would a serpent be offered to him instead (Matthew 7:9–10). 'If you then, who are evil,' Jesus went on, 'know how to give good gifts to your children, how much more will your Father who is in heaven give good things to those who ask him!' (verse 11). As we learn from the parallel verse in Luke, these 'good things' which the Father longs to bestow include the Holy Spirit (Luke 11:13). Jesus taught that the God who feeds the birds of the air will care for us his children, who are of more value than they are (Matthew 6:26). He knows what we need even in terms of material provision like food, drink and clothes (verses 31–32). He not only knows: he knows in advance before the request is made (verse 8). In other words, the fatherhood of God implies that he is prepared to give the very best he has to those who will receive it. And even those who refuse his mercies and spurn his love do not forfeit his fatherly concern. The prodigal in the distant land was still a son and when he returned, the father lavished on him all the tokens of affection and delight – the robe, the ring, the shoes, the calf (Luke 15:22–23).

The same emphasis on God's abundant and undeserved generosity recurs elsewhere in the New Testament at the mention of his fatherhood:

Blessed be the God and Father of our Lord Jesus Christ, who has blessed us in Christ with every spiritual blessing in the heavenly places (Ephesians 1:3).

Blessed be the God and Father of our Lord Jesus Christ! By his great mercy we have been born anew to a living hope through the resurrection of Jesus Christ from the dead, and to an inheritance which is imperishable, undefiled, and unfading, kept in heaven for you (1 Peter 1:3–4).

For this reason I bow my knees before the Father, from whom every family in heaven and on earth is named, that according to the riches of his glory he may grant you to be strengthened with might through his Spirit in the inner man (Ephesians 3:14–16).

As our Father, God is the one who has resources sufficient to match all his children's needs, to equip us for his service here on earth, and to prepare us for an eternity of praise.

# 8

# THE NATURE OF GOD

So far we have been finding out who God is mainly by looking at the names he bears. Of these, the most distinctive is Father. The eternal, almighty, sovereign Lord of the universe is also the one who cares for his children and liberally supplies all their needs. What the Bible says about God in terms of the names which are ascribed to him reaches its climax in what Jesus taught about how we may come to know his Father as our Father too.

Bearing in mind that everything else we learn about God in Scripture is to be interpreted in the light of his fatherhood, we must now go on to catalogue what have usually been regarded as the attributes of God. The traditional language is not in itself biblical, nor is it really very satisfactory, and there are many today who would question whether we can justifiably retain it.

Perhaps the most straightforward alternative is to talk instead about the qualities which the Bible sees in God. They are part of himself and not what human thought has tacked on to him, as it were. We only know about them at all through revelation, but what we can grasp of them is necessarily limited by our imperfect understanding.

In the past, several methods of classification have been devised as these attributes or qualities of God have been under discussion. The simplest and most helpful is to start with the nature of God – what he is in himself apart from any relation to other beings. These are his essential qualities which cannot be passed on, as distinct from those relative qualities which in his grace he stoops to share with us. Such a classification is far from foolproof, but it does at least enable us to begin by contemplating the nature of God as the self-existent one.

## The self-existent one

We cannot begin to imagine what is meant by the fact that God has a life of his own. We are dependent creatures. All that we have and are comes from a source outside ourselves. It is God himself who 'gives to all men life and breath and everything' (Acts 17:25), as Paul told his audience in Athens. God, on the other hand, is altogether independent. It is his very nature to be so. 'The Father has life in himself' (John 5:26). He is the great I AM and, as we have already discovered, that mysterious title implies his self-existence as the one who always was, who still is, and who ever will be (Exodus 3:14).

A story is told about the novelist E. F. Benson. As a young boy he was sent off to bed at an early hour as usual one summer evening. It was still light and he was unable to sleep. He crept to the window and, peeping through a chink in the Venetian blind, he saw his mother on the lawn playing croquet with some people who were strangers to him. The fact that she was entirely unoccupied with him came as an enormous shock to his little mind. He had assumed as a matter of course that she existed solely for him. He had not for a moment realized that she had a life of her own.

This is what the Bible says about God. He is self-existent. He has need of nothing and nobody outside his own being. He is complete in his divine nature. He is not compelled to think of us. The fact that he does so is made all the more remarkable when we realize that it is a matter of love and grace.

## God is spirit

The first quality of God's nature which must engage our attention is *spirituality*. It is this factor which most nearly and fully expresses the essence of the divine. 'God is spirit, and those who worship him must worship in spirit and truth,' Jesus told the Samaritan woman at Jacob's well (John 4:24). 'It is impossible to exhaust the wealth of this great declaration,' wrote Archbishop William Temple. '"God is spirit." That is the most fundamental proposition in theology.' God is not *a* spirit – one among many – any more than he is *a* being. He is spirit and he is being. He is active energy, vibrant with life, and potent with purpose, yet free from the limitations of time and space which are associated with the material. God is the Creator of matter, but never its prisoner.

That is why God is not to be discerned by the bodily senses. He is 'the King of ages, immortal, invisible, the only God' (1 Timothy 1:17). He 'dwells in unapproachable light, whom no man has ever seen or can see' (1 Timothy 6:16). In his essential nature God as spirit is hidden from human view. Only the eyes of faith can see 'him who is invisible', as Moses did (Hebrews 11:27). That makes the incarnation even more incredible, for Christ who came in the flesh is 'the image of the invisible God' (Colossians 1:15).

> God the invisible appears:
> God the blest, the great I AM,
> Sojourns in this vale of tears,
> And Jesus is his name.
> (*Charles Wesley*)

The spirituality of God suggests that, not only in the fact that he is invisible, but in every other respect too his existence is basically different from ours. The contrast between God and man is often expressed in Scripture. He is in heaven, we are on earth (Ecclesiastes 5:2). He is great, we are small. He is strong, we are weak. He is perfect, we are full of faults. That is why Christian thinkers like Søren Kierkegaard could speak about 'the infinite qualitative difference' between God and man. 'The Egyptians are men, and not God; and their horses are flesh, and not spirit' (Isaiah 31:3). 'God is not man, that he should lie, or a son of man, that he should repent [i.e. change his mind]. Has he said, and will he not do it? Or has he spoken, and will he not fulfil it?' (Numbers 23:19).

Although the Bible often refers to God and what he does

in human terms – he sees, he hears, he bares his arm, he stretches out his hand – it must not be supposed that he has a bodily shape. As pure spirit he is not limited in this fashion, and expressions like those quoted above are not to be taken at all literally. God has no eyes, no ears, no arm, no hand. He is spirit, not body. 'Hast thou eyes of flesh? Dost thou see as man sees?' asks Job, and expects the answer no (Job 10:4). The prohibition of idolatry (Exodus 20:4–6) is related to this aspect of God's nature. If he is spirit, then it is not possible to represent him by any visual form.

The spirituality of God also suggests that he enjoys a true and real existence, unhampered by the restrictions and corruption associated with the body. It is noteworthy that in John 4:24 'spirit and truth' (i.e. reality) are connected. In an age when men desperately want to know whether God is real, the appreciation that he is spirit brings healthy reassurance.

## God is infinite

The second quality of God's nature is akin to the first. The Bible speaks not only of his spirituality, but also of his *infinity*. This means that he is not at all hemmed in by circumstances or the imposition of other wills than his own. He is free from any sort of restraint. He is unlimited in his being and character. Only what is contrary to his nature is ruled out.

God's infinity includes his *perfection*. That is, his infinity in relation to himself. His being is complete and flawless. This involves not only the absence of defect but boundless potential as well. Infinite resources are stored up in him. 'Great is the LORD, and greatly to be praised, and his greatness is unsearchable' (Psalm 145:3). In the teaching of Jesus, the divine perfection is set forth as a standard and a stimulus. 'You, therefore, must be perfect, as your heavenly Father is perfect' (Matthew 5:48), or as it is in the New English Bible, 'There must be no limit to your goodness, as your heavenly Father's goodness knows no bounds.'

God's infinity includes his *eternity*. That is his infinity in relation to time. Before time began, he was, and after time ends he will be. 'Thy years will never end' (Hebrews 1:12; cf. Psalm 102:27). Eternity is implied by his name I AM (Exodus 3:14) and (as we have seen) El Olam, the Everlasting (Genesis 21:33). 'Have you not known? Have you not heard? The LORD is the everlasting God, the Creator of the ends of the earth. He does not faint or grow weary' (Isaiah 40:28). God's capacity to renew and re-invigorate his people stems from his eternal nature (verses 29–31).

By the eternity of God, then, the Bible means that God is free from the tedious succession of time and yet contains within himself the cause of time. 'Lord, thou hast been our dwelling place in all generations. Before the mountains were brought forth, or ever thou hadst formed the earth and the world, from everlasting to everlasting thou art God' (Psalm 90:1–2). Because of this 'a thousand years in thy sight are but as yesterday when it is past, or as a watch in the night' (verse 4). Hence the psalmist can address God as the one 'whose years endure throughout all generations' (Psalm 102:24) and who is 'enthroned for ever' (verse 12). To the same eternal God, glory is to be given 'in the church and in Christ Jesus to all generations, for ever and ever. Amen' (Ephesians 3:21).

A recurring title in Isaiah's prophecy is 'the first and the last' (Isaiah 44:6; 48:12; cf. 41:4). He is before all and after all. There was no one and nothing to precede him and there will be no one and nothing to outlast him. It is as the eternal one, the LORD (Yahweh) that he called 'the generations from the beginning' (Isaiah 41:4). It is no accident that in the New Testament the same title of eternity is bestowed on the Lord Jesus Christ (Revelation 1:17).

God's infinity includes his *immensity*. That is his infinity in relation to space. He is above and beyond it, and yet he occupies it all. 'Am I a God at hand, says the LORD, and not a God afar off? Can a man hide himself in secret places so that I cannot see him? says the LORD. Do I not fill heaven and earth? says the LORD' (Jeremiah 23:23–24). There is no corner of this vast universe where he is not.

Yet this does not exhaust his immensity. 'Heaven, even highest heaven, cannot contain him,' as Solomon recognized when he proposed to build the Temple (2 Chronicles 2:6). It seemed almost ridiculous to be planning a house for an infinite God. Yet because of his immensity, the God who is everywhere can also be anywhere and thus 'dwell indeed with man on the earth' (2 Chronicles 6:18).

## God is unchangeable

The third quality of God's nature of which the Bible speaks is his *immutability* or unchangeableness. He remains always the same and therefore can be relied on. Man is sometimes up and sometimes down. We are never quite sure in what mood we will find our fellow humans. But God has no ups and downs. He is constant and dependable. 'For I the LORD do not change; therefore you, O sons of Jacob, are not consumed' (Malachi 3:6). God stands by his covenant despite the rebellion of his people.

According to James, 'every good endowment and every perfect gift is from above, coming down from the Father of lights with whom there is no variation or shadow due to change' (James 1:17). There is probably a topical allusion here to popular astrology. In the first century, as in ours, there were those who looked to the stars to trace their destiny. James explains that Christians prefer to consult the God who made the stars. They may change: he does not. They are liable to parallax (a technical term is employed by the apostle) or eclipse, but God does not alter. He is eternally the same. No shadow of inconsistency ever falls across his nature. He 'does not change like shifting shadows' (James 1:17, New International Version). Indeed, he cannot for his nature is immutable.

Even when all else has been removed, God remains the same. Heaven and earth will disappear; time will be no more, but he will abide. 'Of old thou didst lay the foundation of the earth, and the heavens are the work of thy hands. They will perish, but thou dost endure; they will all wear out like a garment.

Thou changest them like raiment, and they pass away; but thou art the same ...' (Psalm 102:25–27; cf. Hebrews 1:10–12). Notice the practical conclusion drawn by the psalmist in view of God's immutability: 'The children of thy servants shall dwell secure; their posterity shall be established before thee' (Psalm 102:28). Because God is the same (literally it is 'Thou art he'), then his mercy will extend as far as the future itself. The man who trusts in him has nothing to fear.

Because God is not subject to change his is always a fully developed life. Fulfilment is not a goal yet to be achieved. It is eternally realized. There is no growth in God. There is no increase or decrease, no improvement or deterioration. All other forms of life progress towards maturity. God alone is always complete. In the language of philosophy, he is absolute being, and never mere becoming. What he is, he always has been and will be. He is not himself part of the process, as some recent philosophers and even theologians have surmised. He stands outside it as its controller, but is in no sense altered by it.

The spiritual emphasis on God's immutability should not, however, lead us to envisage him as immobile. He is never static. The *living God* – and this is one of the most frequent ways of describing him – is free and flexible in all his actions, capable of adapting himself to meet all kinds of situations. Although he remains essentially the same, he displays an infinite variety in his dealings. For this reason Professor John MacQuarrie of Oxford thinks that a better and more biblical term than immutable or even consistent would be faithful. That stands for God's unchangeableness in the midst of change, and yet leaves ample room for manoeuvre. 'Know therefore that the LORD your God is God, the faithful God' (Deuteronomy 7:9; cf. Isaiah 49:7). 'The steadfast love of the LORD never ceases, his mercies never come to an end; they are new every morning; great is thy faithfulness' (Lamentations 3:22–23).

## God is all-sufficient

A single word sums up the nature of God: it is the word

sufficient. He has within himself all the resources necessary to his own being and to our being too. He never requires help from outside. He is self-contained. There is nothing in his nature which is not himself, and nothing beyond it which is not derived from him. To him alone belongs what the Bible calls 'all the fullness of God' (Ephesians 3:19).

This immeasurable sufficiency is always his but can nevertheless be ours in Christ, in whom 'all the fullness of God was pleased to dwell' (Colossians 1:19; cf. 2:9–10). Out of his limitless resources God can assure his children: 'My grace is sufficient for you' (2 Corinthians 12:9). 'Not that we are competent of ourselves to claim anything as coming from us,' we would hasten to add with the apostle Paul; 'Our competence is from God' (2 Corinthians 3:5).

# 9

# THE MIND OF GOD

In chapters 9–11 of his letter to the Christians in Rome, the apostle Paul wrestles with the problem raised by Israel's rejection of the Messiah. He seeks to justify the ways of God to men as he handles the profound mysteries of election and predestination. He moves beyond the immediate issue of Israel's failure to recognize the Lord Jesus as the Christ, and touches once again on the central theme of the whole epistle – namely, that being right with God is the outcome of saving faith.

As he reaches the close of his argument, Paul bursts into a full-throated ascription of praise: 'O the depth of the riches and wisdom and knowledge of God! How unsearchable are his judgments and how inscrutable his ways!' (Romans 11:33). Then he goes on to ask, 'For who has known the mind of the Lord, or who has been his counsellor?' (verse 34). Two passages from the Old Testament are brought together here, as Paul shows how unfathomable is the mind of God (Isaiah 40:13; Job 41:11). He links the same quotations in 1 Corinthians 2:16 – '"For who has known the mind of the Lord so as to instruct him?" But we have the mind of Christ.'

God, then, has a mind. He thinks and knows. He plans and devises. He determines the course he will take. He controls and orchestrates the whole complex scheme of history. God is the mind behind the universe. Indeed, he is the Mastermind.

In the Old Testament there is no specific word for mind. Heart, soul and spirit are all called in to do duty. The references are invariably to the human mind, however, and, if we are to learn about the mind of God, we need to look at such terms as knowledge, wisdom and understanding. The superiority of the divine mind over the human is everywhere assumed in Scripture. 'For my thoughts are not your thoughts, neither are your ways my ways, says the LORD. For as the heavens are higher than the earth, so are my ways higher than your ways and my thoughts than your thoughts' (Isaiah 55:8–9).

We have already begun to consider the attributes or qualities of God. We started by singling out those which belong to his essential nature, and which mark him off from man in that they cannot be communicated. In this and succeeding chapters we must proceed to examine those attributes and qualities of God which are relative, and therefore can be passed on to man. These again are often classified as intellectual and moral, and it is with the first category that we are at present concerned as we deal with the mind of God. We will enquire what the Bible says about his knowledge, wisdom and truth.

## God's knowledge

'Will any teach God knowledge, seeing that he judges those that are on high?' asked Job (Job 21:22). He felt that his friends, with their pretentious arguments, were really claiming to be smarter than God himself. If God decides the destiny even of the angels, surely he can handle the affairs of men. His knowledge far surpasses that of even the most brilliant human mind. That is an emphasis we need to note today, when man in his arrogance even presumes that he is capable of deciding whether there is a God and, if he recognizes such a being at all, tends to cut him down to pigmy size.

## Different from human knowledge

There are at least four ways in which God's knowledge differs from man's.

(1) It is *complete*. What God knows he knows fully and perfectly, and there is nothing he does not know. Man only knows

in part (1 Corinthians 13:12) and his ignorance always exceeds his knowledge. That is to say, for him there is far more to be known than he now knows. With God there is no ignorance at all. His knowledge is exhaustive: it includes everything about everything. If a man gives the impression that he is a know-all, then he is rightly regarded with suspicion. God really does know all and as a consequence what he knows can never be supplemented or improved. He is, as Scripture teaches, 'perfect in knowledge' (Job 37:16).

(2) God's knowledge differs from man's in that it is *eternal*. It extends beyond time. He knows all that has been, all that is, and all that will be or could be. Man's knowledge is confined to time. He is aware of the present, he can trace something of the past and hazard a guess about the future. But, at its best, what man knows is strictly limited. It appears microscopic indeed compared with God's eternal knowledge.

Moreover, with God it is always now, so that his knowledge is always contemporary. 'Where were you when I laid the foundation of the earth?' the Lord enquires of Job. 'Tell me, if you have understanding. Who determined its measurements – surely you know!' (Job 38:4–5). That is the language of teasing irony, for man clearly does not know because he was not there. God was there and, what is more, in a profound sense he is still there.

(3) God's knowledge differs from man's in that it is *certain*. It allows neither for doubt nor error. It is assured knowledge. What man knows is largely tentative. He can only see things from a limited human perspective. Only God can scan the whole field of enquiry and only he knows with absolute certainty. His is accurate and reliable knowledge. This unambiguous confidence includes what God knows about the choices men make and the way events will turn out. More than that, he even knows what might happen in given circumstances.

When David had captured the fortress of Keilah from the Philistines, he was afraid lest the inhabitants might betray him to Saul. So he enquired of the LORD, 'Will the men of Keilah surrender me and my men into the hand of Saul?' (1 Samuel 23:12). We read that the Lord knew that they would do so, and David was thus enabled to escape. Certainty can hardly go further than that. God not only knows which way the cookie will crumble, he even knows what the alternative would be.

(4) God's knowledge differs from man's in that it is *inborn*. It is not acquired by learning. It belongs to himself. It is intuitive and immediate. Most of what man knows he has to be taught or find out by research. Little by little he builds on what is already known, and thus advances from less to more (Isaiah 28:10). God, on the other hand, never has to learn. He knows because he is a knowing God.

Having spelled out the fundamental difference between divine and human knowledge, we must next analyse what the Bible says about the precise areas included in what God knows. These same passages will also serve to confirm the distinctions outlined above.

## Areas of God's knowledge

(a) God's knowledge covers *himself*. He knows his own being. Self-knowledge is implied by the title 'I AM' as well as the fact that he has revealed himself to man. The fullness of such knowledge cannot be conveyed to finite human minds, but as much as may be known is made available. Even by revelation, man will never come to know all there is to know about God, yet the fact that anything can be disclosed at all presupposes God's perfect self-awareness. If he did not know himself, he would not be able to make himself known.

God's self-knowledge is total. There are no gaps in what he knows about himself. The Holy Spirit is the focus and medium of this comprehensive awareness. 'For the Spirit searches everything, even the depths of God. For what person knows a man's thoughts except the spirit of the man which is in him? So also no one comprehends the thoughts of God except the Spirit of God' (1 Corinthians 2:10–11). The Spirit knows God from the inside, as it were.

(b) God's knowledge covers *creation*. He knows all that is going on in the universe. Nothing is hidden from him. 'For he looks to the ends of the earth, and sees everything under the heavens' (Job 28:24). When in the beginning he created all that is, 'then he saw it and declared it; he established it, and searched it out' (verse 27). Significantly, after the psalmist has explained that in his greatness the Lord 'determines the number of the stars' and 'gives to all of them their names' (Psalm 147:4), he adds that he is not only 'abundant in power', but that 'his understanding is beyond measure' (verse 5).

God knows every living creature he has created from the least to the largest. 'I know all the birds of the air, and all that moves in the field is mine' (Psalm 50:11). 'Who provides for the raven its prey, when its young ones cry to God, and wander about for lack of food?' the Lord asks Job (38:41), and the answer, of course, is that he does so himself. Not even a sparrow alights or touches down on the ground – that may well be the meaning, rather than 'falls to the ground' – without God knowing and indeed permitting it (Matthew 10:29).

(c) God's knowledge covers *man*. He knows all about each individual every moment of their lives. 'Does he not see my ways, and number all my steps?' Job enquires, and is sure that he does (Job 31:4; cf. 34:21). He even keeps count of the times we turn and toss in our sleep (Psalm 56:8), as well as of each hair on our head (Matthew 10:30). No detail is too trivial to escape God's notice.

There is nothing superficial about God's knowledge of man. He searches our minds and hearts (Psalm 7:9; cf. Jeremiah 11:20; 17:10) and reads our most secret thoughts and motives (Psalm 44:21; 139:2). 'Lord, all my longing is known to thee,' the psalmist confesses, 'my sighing is not hidden from thee' (Psalm 38:9). Although a man's conduct may be faultless in his own eyes, 'the LORD weighs the spirit' (Proverbs 16:2). He is indeed the 'watcher of men' (Job 7:20).

(d) God's knowledge covers the *future*. He knows all that it holds. He declares 'the end from the beginning and from ancient times things not yet done' (Isaiah 46:10). He anticipated Pharaoh's refusal to let his people go from Egypt (Exodus 3:19). He gives advance notice of his intentions to his servants the prophets (Amos 3:7). He challenges the bogus deities of the nations surrounding Israel to prove their mettle by forecasting future events. 'Tell us what is to come hereafter, that we may know that you are gods' (Isaiah 41:23). It was God who 'stirred up one from the north' (verse 25) – that is, Cyrus the Great, the Persian monarch, to release the exiled Jews and facilitate their return to their land; and, moreover, he had plainly announced it all before ever it happened. 'Who declared it from the beginning, that we might know, and beforetime, that we might say, "He is right"?' (Isaiah 41:26). Not one of the gods of whom the Gentiles boasted: only the one true God who knows every item that the blueprint of the future contains, for he has drawn it up himself. Such is the comprehensiveness of the divine knowledge. 'Nothing in all creation is hidden from God's sight. Everything is uncovered and laid bare before the eyes of him to whom we must give account' (Hebrews 4:13, New International Version).

In expounding what the Bible tells us about the mind of God we have concentrated on divine knowledge. We must deal more briefly with two kindred examples of God's intellectual qualities – his wisdom and truth.

## God's wisdom

In Romans 11:33 Paul makes a distinction between the wisdom and the knowledge of God. Although related, they are not the same. Wisdom is named first, as it is also in Colossians 2:3, where it is said that in Christ 'are hid all the treasures of wisdom and knowledge'. Put simply, knowledge is a matter of information. It is what might be fed into a computer. Wisdom is the ability to apply knowledge to whatever project may be in hand. Knowledge is theoretical: wisdom is practical. Wisdom has to do with adapting means to ends. As an attribute of God, it means that he is always able to achieve his objectives. He produces the best possible results by using the best possible methods to promote his glory. 'With God are wisdom and might; he has counsel and understanding' (Job 12:13). 'Whence then comes wisdom? And where is the place of understanding? It is hid from the eyes of all living, and concealed from the birds of the air. Abaddon and Death say, "We have heard a rumour of it with our ears." God understands the way to it, and he knows its place' (Job 28:20–23). The wisdom of God so far surpasses any that man may claim to display that the apostle Paul can dismiss it as empty foolishness by comparison (1 Corinthians 1:20).

The wisdom of God is evident in the realms both of nature and of grace. 'O LORD, how manifold are thy works! In wisdom hast thou made them all' (Psalm 104:24). The universe, with all its intricacies and complexities, is an enduring tribute to God's capacity to bend his infinite knowledge to the practical task of creating and sustaining matter and life at every level.

> In all his mighty works
> Amazing wisdom shines!
>> (*Isaac Watts*)

But what is abundantly apparent in nature is even more impressively reflected in the area of redemption. The gospel is the product of God's wise design. It was 'in the wisdom of God' that 'the world did not know God through wisdom' (1 Corinthians 1:21). Behind the inability of man to reach an apprehension of God through the exercise of his rational faculties, lies the calculated purpose of God to bring him to the point where he is prepared to abandon his clever speculations and accept God's way of apparent foolishness in the message of the cross. Hence man attains another sort of wisdom – 'not a wisdom of this age or of the rulers of this age, who are doomed to pass away' but 'a secret and hidden wisdom of God, which God decreed before the ages for our glorification' (1 Corinthians 2:6–7).

It is in the plan of salvation through the death of Christ that the wisdom of God reaches its glorious climax. No one except 'the only wise God' (Romans 16:27) is able to make our standing sure in the gospel of his Son (verse 25). Nothing but his wisdom could bring his purpose to its consummation in the fullness of time, when he will unite (or head up) all things in Christ both in heaven and on earth (Ephesians 1:9–10).

## God's truth

Truth is not simply an attribute of God: it is his very being. He not only exhibits truth in all his words and dealings. He is truth. Twice over in 1 John 5:20 God is described as 'him who is true'. 'And we know that the Son of God has come and has given us understanding of him who is true; and we are in him who is true, in his Son Jesus Christ.' Then John adds: 'This is the true God and eternal life.' Truth here stands for actuality and integrity. God is the one who is real and genuine. He is 'the God of truth' (Isaiah 65:16).

God is truth in the sense that he is all that he as God should be. In him the divine ideal is fully realized. In this he stands apart from rival deities who are exposed as false since they cannot live up to the name. Idols are worthless (Psalm 97:7) and therefore not to be worshipped. The Lord above 'is most high over all the earth' and 'exalted far above all gods' (verse 9) and so is deserving of praise (Psalm 147:1).

God is truth also in the sense that he is to be trusted in all his communications. He will never deceive. He never lies (Titus 1:2). It is impossible for him to play false (Hebrews 6:18). Everything that he makes known about himself is so. He is not one to cheat us. He is altogether worthy of the confidence which he calls us to place in him. He will neither fail us nor forsake us (Deuteronomy 31:6, 8; Joshua 1:5; 1 Chronicles 28:20). If wisdom is the practical application of God's knowledge, truth is the guarantee of its authenticity.

# 10

# THE GOODNESS OF GOD

We come now to a consideration of what might well be described as God's character. After reviewing the qualities which belong to his mind, we must devote this and succeeding chapters to aspects of his disposition. These used to be grouped together under the heading of moral attributes – that is, those that reflect the kind of person God is in terms of the way he behaves.

A word needs to be inserted at this point to underline the connection between human conduct and our view of God. 'When God is not,' observed the French writer and philosopher Jean-Paul Sartre in a perceptive comment, 'everything is changed and everything is allowed.' It is by no means accidental that our permissive society today has emerged at a time when the reality of God is being questioned or denied. Morality has its source in God. It is only because the supreme being who governs the universe is a certain sort of person that there are any adequate grounds for setting up standards of behaviour.

To abandon belief in a moral God is to undermine the structure of society, and this has been happening in our time. It was naïvely assumed by some that man can continue to practice Christian virtues even though he has rejected the Christian faith and is a stranger to Christian experience. Such a superficial hypothesis has now been exposed as a fallacy. It is rather like the Cheshire cat in Lewis Carroll's *Alice Through the Looking Glass*. It was in the habit of disappearing, leaving behind nothing but its grin. But the grin without the cat cannot linger for long, and neither can Christian conduct when detached from Christian convictions. According to Pamela

Hansford-Johnson, who investigated the circumstances surrounding the notorious moors murders and wrote a book *On Iniquity*, 'When the Sermon on the Mount was bundled into the dustbin a moral vacuum was created.' That goes a long way to explain the kind of climate in which we live today, when often anything goes as far as morals are concerned.

To find out what the Bible teaches about God's character, then, is to recover the necessary criterion by which human behaviour is to be assessed and controlled. If standards are no more than the conventions of the social group, they are unlikely to survive. They retain their authority only because they reach us from God himself. Nothing could be of greater practical relevance today than to rediscover the positive moral values expressed in the divine character. These include goodness, righteousness, holiness and love. We will deal with the first now, and reserve further and separate chapters for the others.

## The meaning of goodness

The goodness of God is one of the central themes of Scripture. We are invited to 'taste and see that the LORD is good!' (Psalm 34:8) and for this reason to give thanks to his name (Psalm 54:6). 'O how abundant is thy goodness,' exclaims the psalmist (Psalm 31:19), and the prophet Isaiah praises the Lord for his 'great goodness to the house of Israel' (Isaiah 63:7). 'The LORD is good,' declares Nahum, 'a stronghold in the day of trouble; he knows those who take refuge in him' (Nahum 1:7).

In the Old Testament the Hebrew word translated 'good' means, in the first place, that which is pleasant and agreeable, like the fruit on the tree of knowledge in the garden of Eden (Genesis 3:6). Then it comes to signify that which is estimable or upright, reaching a recognized standard. When applied to God, it suggests that he is kind and gracious. 'For thou, O Lord, art good and forgiving, abounding in steadfast love to all who call on thee' (Psalm 86:5).

There are two Greek adjectives in the New Testament for 'good'. The more normal term refers to inner worth, while the other is equivalent to 'beautiful' or 'noble'. The latter is never used of God, although it does characterize Jesus as the good shepherd (John 10:11, 14). One noun translated as goodness is derived from the first of the adjectives and denotes a quality in the Christian (Romans 15:14; Galatians 5:22). The other really means kindness, and is applied both to the Christian (Galatians 5:22) and God (Romans 2:4; 11:22). That is why in some passages where the Authorized Version has goodness, the Revised Standard Version and other modern translations have kindness.

## God alone is all-good

The Bible insists that God alone is all-good. Any goodness in man is not his own, but due to God. Even at best it is imperfect. It is true that 'everything created by God is good' (1 Timothy 4:4), but only in so far as it is his creation. Only God is good in himself and by nature.

A stranger once ran up to Jesus as he was setting out on a journey and, dropping to his knees, asked him, 'Good Teacher, what must I do to inherit eternal life?' (Mark 10:17). Jesus did not disclaim the title, but wanted to know whether the man realized what it implied. 'Why do you call me good? No one is good but God alone' (verse 18). In Matthew 19:17 it is 'One there is who is good' – that is, God. Goodness belongs only to him.

That is a salutary reminder. Too often we are tempted to rely on some alleged goodness of our own to make and keep us right with God. The Bible will have none of that. We have no goodness of our own. It all comes from God. 'What have you that you did not receive?' Paul asks the Christians in Corinth. 'If then you received it, why do you boast as if it were not a gift?' (1 Corinthians 4:7). Equally, when we realize that God alone is all good and the source of all good, we are delivered from envy, for we recognize that any goodness others may possess is not their own but his ( James 3:14, 16; 1 Peter 2:1).

In this insistence that only God is all-good the Bible reverses the idea of goodness entertained by the old Greek philosophers, and adopted by many people today. They thought of the good in abstract terms as a something in itself. From this they argued that man must seek this highest good and that indeed it may be expressed in the form of the divine. As Dr James Packer rightly points out, the biblical writers 'define good in terms of God', and not the other way round. When Scripture declares that God is good it speaks in personal terms. What is meant is that 'God is the Good One'. There is no such thing as 'the good': there is only 'the Good One', from whom all goodness flows.

## God's goodness shown to all

The Bible tells us that God's goodness is shown to all. No one has a monopoly of it. The market of divine goodness can never be cornered. It is available for everyone. 'The LORD is good to all, and his compassion is over all that he has made' (Psalm 145:9). So 'let everything that breathes praise the LORD!' (Psalm 150:6). He is not only all-good: he is good to all.

(1) God is good to *all creatures*. Nothing is neglected. It is he 'who gives food to all flesh' (Psalm 136:25). He helps not only man but beast (Psalm 36:6). He has pity even on cattle (Jonah 4:11). He feeds the birds and clothes the flowers (Matthew 6:26–30). The earth is replete with his steadfast love (Psalm 119:64).

(2) God is good to *all men*. No one is excluded. No one is deprived. God's goodness extends to the whole human race. He waits to be gracious to all. 'The LORD is near to all who call upon him, to all who call upon him in truth. He fulfils the desire of all who fear him, he also hears their cry, and saves them' (Psalm 145:18–19). No one who sincerely looks to him will be refused.

Good Thou art, and good Thou dost,
   Thy mercies reach to all,
Chiefly those who on Thee trust
   And for Thy mercy call.

*(Charles Wesley)*

Yet even those who do not respond to God's overtures of grace, and decline his proffered salvation, nevertheless benefit from his goodness as mediated through the processes of nature. 'He makes his sun rise on the evil and on the good, and sends rain on the just and on the unjust,' as Jesus himself taught (Matthew 5:45).

(3) God is good to *all sinners*. Scripture focuses particular attention on God's attitude to those who remain estranged from him. The gospel is for such. The appeal of the Bible is directed to them in an unmistakable fashion. That is the thrust of the Old Testament. 'As I live, says the Lord GOD, I have no pleasure in the death of the wicked, but that the wicked turn from his way and live; turn back, turn back from your evil ways; for why will you die, O house of Israel?' (Ezekiel 33:11). That is the heart of the New Testament gospel. The Lord 'is very patient . . . because it is not his will for any to be lost, but for all to come to repentance' (2 Peter 3:9, New English Bible). His goodness to sinners is shown above all in his decision to send his Son to die so that they might be reconciled to him (Romans 5:6–10).

(4) God is good to *all believers*. His goodness to us does not exhaust itself in bringing us to salvation. It continues with us throughout our days. 'Surely [or only] goodness and mercy shall follow me all the days of my life; and I shall dwell in the house of the LORD for ever' (Psalm 23: 6). Those who believe in God may confidently expect to 'see the goodness of the LORD in the land of the living' (Psalm 27:13).

Samuel Chadwick, once Principal of Cliff College, used to say that there are no people like God's people. It is they who experience the goodness of God in fullest measure. 'Happy are you, O Israel! Who is like you, a people saved by the LORD, the shield of your help, and the sword of your triumph!' (Deuteronomy 33:29). It is his people and the sheep of his pasture who give thanks to him and bless his name, 'for the LORD is good; his steadfast love endures for ever, and his faithfulness to all generations' (Psalm 100:5).

God's goodness to believers will be proved to all eternity. It extends beyond this present existence and endures for ever. Paul tells the Corinthians that 'what God has prepared for those who love him' is beyond anything that has even been seen or heard or even thought of (1 Corinthians 2:9; cf. Isaiah 64:4; 65:17). But what God had designed far in advance from before the beginning of time to bring us to our full glory (verse 7) has already been revealed to us by the Spirit (verse 10). Such is the goodness of God to those who acknowledge his name.

If we were to complete the picture of the divine goodness which reaches all, we would have to examine some other biblical words like grace, mercy, love, patience and longsuffering. These all introduce aspects of the uniform goodness of God. Later we shall be dealing at length with two of them – grace and love – but in this context we may say that grace is the goodness of God unmerited by men (Titus 3:5; Romans 3:24), mercy is the goodness of God towards men in need of compassion (Luke 1:78–79), love is the goodness of God seeking to restore man to communion with himself (John 3:16; Titus 3:4), whereas patience and longsuffering represent the goodness of God waiting for man's repentance (1 Peter 3:20; 2 Peter 3:9).

When God passed before Moses on Mount Sinai, he characterized himself as 'the LORD, the LORD, a God merciful and gracious, slow to anger, and abounding in steadfast love and faithfulness' (Exodus 34:6). Each of these traits contributes to the overall image of God's goodness as it is displayed to all.

At the outset of this chapter we explained how God and morality are related. The kind of God we worship will be reflected in the way we live and act. If we profess to believe in a God who is good – gracious, merciful, loving, patient and longsuffering – then we must be like this ourselves. Our attachment to him is artificial and even hypocritical unless his goodness is apparent in us. 'Love your enemies,' Jesus commanded, 'and do good, and lend, expecting nothing in return; and your reward will be great, and you will be sons of the Most High; for he is kind to the ungrateful and the selfish. Be merciful, even as your Father is merciful' (Luke 6:35–36).

# 11

## THE HOLINESS OF GOD

Old words are like old coins. They wear out and become smooth with use. Their original currency is obscured and we find it hard to make out what they were intended to convey. A term which was once perfectly clear and unambiguous either becomes quite unintelligible or, worse still, takes on an altogether different connotation.

That is what has happened to 'holy' and 'holiness'. No doubt there was a time when, in an atmosphere more congenial to the appreciation of spiritual realities than ours today, such vital biblical words carried a freight of relevant meaning. But nowadays they make little or no impression. They slide off the modern ear like soap from a narrow bath edge. If they make any impact at all, they recall misleading associations. 'Holy' and 'holiness' smack of sanctimonious piety and smug Pharisaism. We think of holy Joes, and 'Holy Wullie's Prayer' in the poetry of Robert Burns. Holiness is hardly an admired quality in our secular society, and for this reason people are puzzled when it is ascribed to God. They shrink from what they take to be an unattractive image.

We need to banish all such misconceptions from our minds and start with a clean slate as we seek to learn what the Bible teaches about the holiness of God. It is so fundamental that the title 'Holy One' in Scripture is synonymous with God himself. It is thought to require no further explanation, although in the Old Testament 'of Israel' is often added. When, for example, Isaiah refers to the Holy One who is a flame to burn and devour thorns and briers (Isaiah 10:17), or Habakkuk describes how the Holy One came from Mount Paran in the Sinai desert (Habakkuk 3:3), it is obvious not only from the context but even from the designation itself that the prophets are talking about God.

Again, when God says who he is, this is the identification he chooses. 'For I am the LORD your God; consecrate yourselves therefore, and be holy, for I am holy. ... For I am the LORD who brought you up out of the land of Egypt, to be your God; you shall therefore be holy, for I am holy' (Leviticus 11:44, 45). 'I am the LORD' and 'I am holy' amount almost to the same thing. (Cf. Leviticus 19:2; 20:7; 21:8; Joshua 24:19; Psalm 99:5, 9; Hosea 11:9.)

## The meaning of holiness

First, in examining the holiness of God we must define its meaning. The precise significance of the Hebrew root from which the Old Testament vocabulary of holiness stems has been the subject of much discussion and is still not absolutely certain. It is similar to the word for glory and the opposite of common or profane (cf. 1 Samuel 21:5; Ezekiel 22:26; 42:20; 44:23). An earlier theory related it to renewal.

It is generally held, however, that the essence of holiness is *separation* from the secular. The root is thought to be connected with cutting off, withdrawing, or setting apart. That which is holy is removed from common use and is in a class by itself. It is not difficult to see how appropriate such an idea is when related to the nature of God.

Some scholars note a similarity between the Hebrew root and a word in the Akkadian language which stands for what is clear, or brilliant. The concept is allied to that of fear. The shining and the terrible are frequently linked in Scripture, when God makes himself manifest to his people by fire. That is the case in the phenomenon of the burning bush (Exodus 3:2–5), and even more evidently, when the law was given on Mount Sinai (Exodus 19:18). Fire also symbolizes purity, and all these factors – brightness, fearfulness and purity – may well be included in

the meaning of holiness. The basic Old Testament understanding of holy is carried over into the New, where it is
developed in relation to the Son and the Spirit. Arising from
this definition of God's holiness, we may say that it has to do
with his *difference* from man. It is that about him which marks
him off from humanity. It represents his distinctiveness. 'I am
God and not man,' he declares, 'the Holy One in your midst'
(Hosea 11:9). What the theologians call the 'otherness' of God is
implied by his holiness.

It is an axiom of Scripture that holiness is of the Lord. It
belongs to him and to him alone. People, times, places and
objects are made holy only by reason of their association with
him. Nobody and nothing is holy apart from God. He is its
sole source. Holiness is not to be regarded as a quality which
man can ever produce himself. Its divine origin is everywhere
attested.

God's holiness, while emphasizing his incomparability with
any created being, and more particularly his distinction from
man, is not to be interpreted in such a way as to render him
remote. 'For I am God and not man, the Holy One *in your
midst*' (Hosea 11:9). Not only is he other than man: he is also
near to man and concerned about him. This too is an aspect
of his holiness. To equate it only with the fact that God is above
man and to forget that he is also with man and, in the person
of his Son, actually became man, is to fall short of what the
Bible reveals. God is kind, loving and gracious, even though
he is so always as the one who is utterly different from man
in his holiness.

## Holiness as God's selfhood

Holiness, like love, is not merely one of God's attributes. It
represents his essential nature. As we have seen, 'the Holy One'
or 'the Holy One of Israel' stands for God himself. The latter
is the theme song of Isaiah, where it is found no less than
twenty-four times. It does not mean that the Holy One belongs
to Israel. He is so, not because he is dedicated to Israel, but

because he has set aside Israel for himself. He is the Holy One who makes his people holy too. According to Sir George Adam Smith, for Isaiah God is

> the Incomparable, the Unapproachable, the Utter Contrast of man, the Exalted and Sublime. Better expression could not be found for the full idea of Godhead. This little word 'holy' radiates heaven's own breadth of meaning.

We may say holiness is God's selfhood. When he swears by his holiness he swears by himself (Amos 4:2; 6:8). It is an oath he does not really need to repeat, since he is the ever-living One. 'Once for all I have sworn by my holiness' (Psalm 89:35). That is why he can underwrite his assurances with a similar appeal: 'God has promised by his holiness' (Psalm 108:7 margin; the Hebrew could also mean 'in his sanctuary'); 'for he remembered his holy promise' (Psalm 105:42). God seals his guarantees with his personal stamp, for his holiness is nothing less than himself.

The same inference is to be drawn from those passages in which the Lord appeals to his holy name. Both his name and his holiness are really to be interpreted as himself. That is apparent from such a text as Leviticus 22:32–33 – 'And you shall not profane my holy name, but I will be hallowed among the people of Israel; I am the LORD who sanctify you, who brought you out of the land of Egypt to be your God: I am the LORD.' Clearly God's name, God's holiness, and God himself are all interlinked and are to be treated virtually as one.

God is jealous for his holy name, as he is jealous for his own honour and reputation (Ezekiel 39:25). He abhors its desecration when his people fall back into pagan practices, since it is in fact a form of blasphemy against himself (Jeremiah 34:16; Ezekiel 20:39; 36:20; 43:8). He acts in mercy for the sake of his holy name because he is true to himself (Ezekiel 36:21–22). 'And I will vindicate the holiness of my great name, which has been profaned among the nations, and which you have profaned among them; and the nations will know that I am the LORD, says the Lord GOD, when through you I vindicate my holiness before their eyes' (verse 23, cf. 39:7). Hence those who belong to him are to glory in his holy name as in himself (1 Chronicles 16:10; Psalm 105:3). So Mary, in the song called the Magnificat, rejoices in God her Saviour: 'He who is mighty has done great things for me, and holy is his name' (Luke 1:49).

The very first petition in the prayer that Jesus taught his disciples has to do with this same association of holiness with the selfhood of God. 'Pray then like this: Our Father who art in heaven, Hallowed be thy name' (Matthew 6:9). God's name represents his nature. It is himself in so far as he makes himself known. 'Hallow' could mean 'make holy', but not here. It is impossible to make God's name holy, for it already is holy. But 'hallow' may also mean 'regard or treat as holy', which is what we do with respect to God's name when we recognize who he is. However, 'hallow' can be taken in yet another way, as 'make known to be holy'. In prayer we ask that God will reveal more and more of his holiness and himself. We want him to show us who he is, so that we may give him the place in our lives that his divine nature demands.

God's holiness, then, is his self-assertion. It is his declaration of who he is. What proves God to be God is that he is holy. In a graphic sentence Professor Otto Baab has summarized the teaching of the Bible on this subject. 'The "godness" of God is highlighted by the word "holy" when it is used in connection with him.'

## An aspect of God's power

The holiness of God is an aspect of his power. It is as the Holy One that he controls all the forces of the universe. It is noticeable that in Mary's song it is 'he who is mighty' who has done great things, and thus vindicated the holiness of his name (Luke 1:49).

Isaiah warns us against the folly of arguing with God. The man who keeps up a running battle with his Maker is bound to end up a loser. It is as if the clay in the potter's hand were to rise up in protest at what was being made of it, or children should complain to their father that it was his fault that they were as they were. 'Thus says the LORD, the Holy One of Israel, and his Maker: "Will you question me about my children, or command me concerning the work of my hands?"' (Isaiah 45:11). God's holiness is the sign of his authority. It reminds us that he is in charge, not only of the universe, but of us.

We must not think of him, however, as a tyrant who gets a kick out of keeping us in order and wielding the big stick. His aim is not to let us know who is boss and make sure that we jump to attention, though we should. It is rather that he may bless us and do us good. God's power is not exercised in any exhibitionist fashion. It is all directed to fulfil the purposes of grace.

The Bible goes out of its way to make it clear that all God is and does focuses on his plan of salvation. The power of God is supremely displayed in the gospel (Romans 1:16). We tend to think that the most impressive indications of divine power are to be found in God's control of physical energy. The Bible sees the greatest miracle in his ability to transform sinful man into a new creation in Christ Jesus (2 Corinthians 5:17).

In the prophecy of Isaiah, the recurring title 'the Holy One of Israel' is more than once linked with the theme of redemption. The immediate allusion is to the release of the nation from exile in Babylon, but the emancipation of the individual from the bondage of sin, which was to be realized in Christ, is also anticipated. 'Thus says the LORD, your Redeemer, the Holy One of Israel: "For your sake I will send to Babylon and break down all the bars, and the shouting of the Chaldeans will be turned to lamentations. I am the LORD, your Holy One, the Creator of Israel, your King"' (Isaiah 43:14–15). 'The Redeemer of Israel' and 'the Holy One' are identified in Isaiah 49:7 and 54:5, and in Isaiah 43:3 it is 'the Holy One of Israel, your Saviour'.

The holiness of God as an aspect of his power is also expressed in terms of his *justice*. It is he who maintains among his people what nowadays we call law and order, and administers discipline. He has the right to do this as the Holy One. 'The LORD is great in Zion; he is exalted over all the peoples. Let them praise

thy great and terrible name! Holy is he! Mighty King, lover
of justice, thou hast established equity; thou hast executed
justice and righteousness in Jacob. Extol the LORD our God;
worship at his footstool! Holy is he!' (Psalm 99:2–5). According
to Isaiah, 'the LORD of hosts is exalted in justice, and the Holy
God shows himself holy in righteousness' (Isaiah 5:16).

God's role as a dispenser of justice is not confined to his
dealings with his people Israel. His authority is exercised over
the Gentile nations as well. The only passage in the Old Testament which singles out Sidon for treatment, independently of
its stronger partner Tyre, is found at the end of Ezekiel 28.
The prophet rounds off a series of oracles directed against these
two Phoenician cities with a warning to Sidon: 'Thus says the
Lord GOD: "Behold, I am against you, O Sidon, and I will
manifest my glory in the midst of you. And they shall know
that I am the LORD when I execute judgments in her, and
manifest my holiness in her"' (Ezekiel 28:22).

In Ezekiel 38 there is a similar indictment of Gog, the ruler
of Magog, probably situated between Cappadocia and Media
in Asia Minor. When he dares to attack the land of Israel, the
Lord's wrath will be aroused and Gog will suffer an ignominious
defeat. From the book of the Revelation, we learn that Gog
and Magog represent the godless nations of the world who at
the end of the age will gang up against God's people (Revelation 20:8). 'I will summon every kind of terror against Gog,
says the Lord GOD; every man's sword will be against his
brother. With pestilence and bloodshed I will enter into
judgment with him. ... So I will show my greatness and my
holiness and make myself known in the eyes of many nations.
Then they will know that I am the LORD' (Ezekiel 38:21–23).

## God's attitude to sin

The holiness of God also manifests itself in his attitude to sin.
It denotes not merely his own separation from sin in the perfection of his own being, but his abhorrence of it and hostility
to it as one who is 'of purer eyes than to behold evil' and who

cannot 'look on wrong' (Habakkuk 1:13). He himself is 'a God of faithfulness and without iniquity' (Deuteronomy 32:4), and as such he is unable to condone or ignore sin in others. He hates the evil that men devise in their hearts against one another and against himself (Zechariah 8:17). When he sent 'his own Son in the likeness of sinful flesh and for sin, he condemned sin in the flesh' (Romans 8:3).

As God is sinless by nature, and thus alone is holy in the full sense of the word, so, on the contrary, all mankind 'have sinned and fall short of the glory of God' (Romans 3:23). 'There is none holy like the LORD' (1 Samuel 2:2). As Bildad the Shuhite confessed, 'Behold, even the moon is not bright and the stars are not clean in his sight; how much less man, who is a maggot, and the son of man, who is a worm!' (Job 25:5–6). Even the angels are not holy as God is. How then may any human claim to be so? 'Can mortal man be righteous before [or more than] God? Can a man be pure before [or more than] his Maker? Even in his servants he puts no trust, and his angels he charges with error; how much more those who dwell in houses of clay' (Job 4:17–19).

When confronted by the holiness of God, our sin grows self-conscious. That was the experience of Isaiah. In his vision he saw the exalted Lord and heard the heavenly choir chanting, 'Holy, holy, holy is the LORD of hosts; the whole earth is full of his glory' (Isaiah 6:3). His immediate reaction was to acknowledge his own impurity. 'Woe is me! For I am lost; for I am a man of unclean lips, and I dwell in the midst of a people of unclean lips' (verse 5). In the presence of God's holiness he became aware, not only of his own sin, but of that of all mankind, for in this respect Israel was a sample of the entire human race.

The highest expression of God's holiness, however, is in his love. In the Old Testament, it is in the prophecy of Hosea that this is most clearly brought out. Hosea married a wife called Gomer who then left him not just for another man but for other men (Hosea 2:5). The prophet's own domestic tragedy was turned into a parable. This is what God has to put up with from his faithless people. Hosea still loved his wife and was ready to receive her back. So God's holiness, as the sum of his being, contains the creative love which tears and yet heals, strikes but also binds us up (Hosea 6:1).

He cannot approve of sin, and must meet it with reproof and punishment. 'For thou art not a God who delights in wickedness; evil may not sojourn with thee' (Psalm 5:4). Nevertheless, even while he shows his displeasure with sin, he continues to love the sinner. Both these attitudes are reflections of his holiness. Because he is holy, he hates evil. Because he is holy, he never stops loving.

The revelation of God as holy love reaches its fullness in Christ and in the Scriptures of the New Testament. It is to this evidence that we must next give our attention.

# 12

# THE LOVE OF GOD

There are three words recorded in the first letter of John which say everything that we really need to know about God. They are so important that they are repeated, in case we should find them apparently so simple that we might be inclined to overlook the depth of meaning they contain. In chapter 4 we read: 'God is love' (verse 8). And again in the middle of verse 16 the same assertion recurs: 'God is love.' 'He who does not love does not know God; for God is love' (verse 8). 'So we know and believe the love God has for us. God is love, and he who abides in love abides in God, and God abides in him' (verse 16).

As Emil Brunner has said, the message that God is love represents something altogether novel in the world. We see how true this is if we try to apply the statement to the various religions of mankind. Wotan is love; Zeus is love; Jupiter, Brahma, Vishnu, Allah is love. None of these fits. Even the god of Plato, who is the principle of all good, is not love. So Brunner concludes that this affirmation 'is the supreme point of the biblical revelation alone, and only in this connexion is it possible and intelligible'.

God is love. That is indeed the high-water mark of what is made known to us about our Maker. Nothing more and nothing loftier and nothing better can be said. God cannot exist without loving. Love is his very essence. To speak of God is to speak of love and to speak of love in its truest meaning is to speak of God.

This is something which goes beyond the declaration that 'love is of [or from] God' (verse 7), although that of course is true. It is something more than an assertion that God loves, although indeed he does. 'God loves' is equivalent to announcing that God creates, God rules, or God judges. It would simply suggest that loving is but one of his activities.

When we learn, however, that God is love, we are being told that all his activity is love. There is nothing he does which is not in love. When he creates, he creates in love. When he rules, he rules in love. When he judges, he judges in love. He cannot be God without love. That is his name and that is his nature. We must never think of his holiness, his sovereignty, his justice, his severity, his wrath, apart from love. Nor must we think of his love apart from his holiness, his sovereignty, his justice, his severity, and his wrath. His love is holy love and his holiness is loving holiness. His love is sovereign and his sovereignty is loving. His justice, severity and even his wrath are always exercised in love, and his love is not to be divorced from his justice, severity and wrath lest it should degenerate into senti- mentality. A lot of loose and dangerous nonsense has been said and written about the love of God. If we are to avoid it, we need to maintain the balance that Scripture provides.

## The essence of God's love

We must first think about the essence of God's love. What exactly is it as the Bible understands it? It lies in utter self- giving for the sake of others. It has been said that there are two kinds of love – the love which receives and the love which bestows. The former gloats over the sacrifice it obtains, the second delights in the sacrifice it makes. Only the latter is recognizable as the love we see in God, and which he wants to see in us. It is the love that is different. It is so different that the New Testament has to mint a special word for it.

In the first-century world, which was not unlike our per- missive society today, love was linked principally with sex in the minds of most people. *Eros* – from which we get the word 'erotic' – was the commonest term for love, often meaning no more than sensual lust. And yet, although so widespread in its use, it does not occur in the New Testament, 'for it is a shame even to speak of the things that they do in secret' (Ephesians 5:12).

Another word, *philia*, is more respectable and has to do with normal friendship. It is found in James 4:4 with reference to that conformity to the world which is a sign of hostility to God (cf. Romans 12:2). A combination of *philia* and *adelphos* (a brother) produces the portmanteau word *philadelphia*, or brotherly love, which is found several times in the New Testament. Yet another Greek term (*storge*) stood for family affection.

This vocabulary, however, was totally inadequate to express the love of God. There was nothing in the standard dictionary to do justice to it. What was required was a virtually new coinage to denote the selfless, sacrificial love of God. Under the tuition of the Holy Spirit the biblical writers were led to adopt the special word *agape*. It did already exist on a few inscriptions, but there is no clear instance of it in literature outside Christianity. In the Septuagint it was employed to translate the Hebrew *chesed* (steadfast love) which has been defined as 'a spontaneous feeling which leads to self-giving'.

*Agape*, then, is love which longs to give rather than to get. It is the love that seeks only the good of others and has no thought of its own satisfaction. This is the essence of God's love. He so loved that he gave – and did not even spare his only Son (John 3:16; Romans 8:32).

## The ground of God's love

We must think next about the ground of God's love. It is based on his very nature. It rests on himself and its springboard is the fact that he is love.

It is the love of God and no other that is commended to us at the cross, and in its rendering of Romans 5:8, the New International Version brings that out. 'But God demonstrates his own love for us in this: While we were still sinners, Christ died for us.' God's love arises from within. It is not prompted from outside himself. 'God first loved us,' declared Calvin, 'without being prompted to it beforehand by our love.' In other words, God's love is not a response to ours. Our love is a response to his. 'We love, because he first loved us' (1 John 4:19). God does not need the stimulus of our love to spur him on to love us. We need the stimulus of his love to spur us on to love him.

Jesus taught that God loves us as a heavenly Father. A father loves his child before ever that child can start to love him. Moreover, God is initially and most significantly the 'Father of our Lord Jesus Christ' (Romans 15:6). The love of God finds an object within the Godhead. He is eternal love because he loves eternally. 'The Father loves the Son,' said Jesus, 'and shows him all that he himself is doing' (John 5:20). What was so when our Lord was here on earth in a man's body, had been so from all eternity and will be so to endless ages. Love has always existed between the Father and the Son. The love the Son has for us comes from the same source as the love the Father has. 'As the Father has loved me, so have I loved you; abide in my love' (John 15:9).

When we look for the reason why God loves, it cannot be located anywhere but in himself. There is certainly nothing of worth in the object of his love as it reaches confused, frustrated, selfish, sinful man. In ourselves we are altogether undeserving. We do not love others, yet he loves us. His is 'love to the loveless shown', as Samuel Crossman puts it in a seventeenth-century hymn.

In reminding the Israelites that they were picked out as a people for God's possession from among all the nations on earth, Moses sought to ascertain the reason why. 'It was not because you were more in number than any other people that the LORD set his love upon you and chose you, for you were the fewest of all peoples' (Deuteronomy 7:7). It was nothing to do with their numerical strength or any other advantage they might appear to enjoy. The reason lay not in what they were but in who God was. 'But it is because the LORD loves you, and is keeping the oath which he swore to your fathers' (verse 8). The ground of God's love is in his own nature. He loves because he is love.

An old and once popular party game requires each participant to supply an alphabetical reason for love. 'I love my love with an A because . . .' – and then must follow a word beginning with that letter – because he is admirable, because he is amiable, because he is ambitious, and so on. The game proceeds right through to Z – 'I love my love with a B because', 'I love my love with a C because.' It is assumed that there is a reason for love, and that that reason is to be sought in some quality displayed by the beloved.

God's love has no 'because' outside himself. He does not love us for what we are, but only through who he is. 'To the question: Why does God love? there is only one right answer,' declares Bishop Anders Nygren, the Swedish theologian who has made this theme his own. 'Because it is his nature to love.' The Bible gets no further than saying that it is 'for his name's sake' (Psalm 79:9; 106:8) – that is, because he is who he is.

## The aim of God's love

We go on to think about the aim of God's love. It has to do entirely with the welfare of those he loves and not in the least with any desire for self-gratification. God does not love, as we so often do, in order to feel a glow of fulfilment. He loves only because he longs to share himself with others. The love of God is his urge to impart himself and all the benefits he can bring, to those who without him will never experience the full potential of life.

God's love is distinguished from human love in that there is nothing selfishly possessive about it. God is not concerned to add us to his property, as it were, for we are his already. He is only interested in our well-being, for he knows that he is the key to it. 'Thou dost show me the path of life,' testifies the psalmist; 'in thy presence there is fullness of joy, in thy right hand are pleasures for evermore' (Psalm 16:11). It is in his love that God makes every possible provision for all to enjoy the exhilarating prospects that open up for those who enter into new and lasting life in Christ.

The fifth chapter of Isaiah's prophecy opens with a love song. It may have been sung at a harvest feast. It tells about the beloved and the vineyard he owned high up on a usually fertile hillside. He did all that could be done to make it productive. No item was overlooked. He dug it over thoroughly and cleared it of stones. He planted only the best red vines. He built a watchtower from which to look out for prowling beasts or marauding men. He hewed out a winepress in it as he anticipated a plentiful crop of grapes. But instead, to his chagrin and disappointment, it yielded nothing but tiny, bitter, dry, wild berries. He asked a pertinent question: 'What more was there to do for my vineyard, that I have not done in it?' (Isaiah 5:4).

That is a parable of God's love. It has a New Testament counterpart in one of the tales that Jesus told as recorded in Luke 13:6–9. The aim of divine love is to do the very best that can be done for every person. It seeks to create the most helpful conditions possible for their growth in grace. The pathos of the situation, as in Isaiah's love song, lies in the fact that so often God is grieved because no suitable fruit appears.

## The scope of God's love

Like his goodness, God's love extends to all. No one is left out. The circle of divine love embraces all mankind. The answer to the question 'Whom does God love?' is 'Everybody without exception.' That indeed is the assurance of the gospel. We can tell anyone and everyone, 'God loves you.'

The apostle Paul reminds the Ephesians about the comprehensiveness of God's love. 'But God, who is rich in mercy, out of the great love with which he loved us, even when we were dead through our trespasses, made us alive together with Christ (by grace you have been saved)' (Ephesians 2:4–5). Some punctuate the verse so as to combine 'even when we were dead' with 'made us alive together in Christ', but this is to underline the obvious fact that only the dead can be brought to life. The closer association in the sentence is between 'the great love with which he loved us' and 'even when we were dead through our trespasses'.

That is an astonishing disclosure indeed. Pity the man who rejects such love. God does not wait for us to improve before his love is offered to us. It reaches us when we need it most – when we are sunk in sin. 'God shows his love for us in that while we were yet sinners Christ died for us' (Romans 5:8). If, then, God's love is directed to those who are still deep in their sins, without a spark of spiritual life, it is a love meant for all, since this is the plight of every man in his natural state. Sin is universal and, if it is to meet our need, God's love must be universal too. If it could miss anyone out, how can a seeker be sure that he is not left in the cold? But God's love *is* universal, and in that we can rejoice.

# FURTHER READING

From a long list of books about various aspects of God, his character and activities, the following represent a comprehensive sample.

John Baillie, *Our Knowledge of God* (Oxford University Press 1963; reprinted from 1939).
John Baillie, *The Sense of the Presence of God* (Oxford University Press 1962).
Herman Bavinck, *The Doctrine of God* (Banner of Truth 1977; reprinted from Eng. trans. 1951).
Helmut Gollwitzer, *The Existence of God as Confessed by Faith* (Westminster Press, Eng. trans. 1964).
James I. Packer, *Knowing God* (Hodder and Stoughton 1973).
A. W. Pink, *The Sovereignty of God* (Banner of Truth 1961).
Francis A. Schaeffer, *The God Who is There* (Hodder and Stoughton 1968).
D. W. D. Shaw, *Who is God?* (SCM Press 1968).
John W. Wenham, *The Goodness of God* (Inter-Varsity Press 1974).

# INDEX